SALUKI
COMPANION OF KINGS

Saluki

Companion of Kings

Vera H. Watkins
WINDSWIFT SALUKIS

— FENROSE —

*First Edition 1974
Published by Fenrose Limited,
21 Mount Ephraim Road,
Tunbridge Wells, Kent.*

*Typesetting by Amigo Graphics Centre, Ltd.
Printed photolitho in Great Britain by
Ebenezer Baylis & Son Limited,
The Trinity Press, Worcester and London.*

*1974 Vera Watkins
ISBN 0 903879 10 7*

Contents

Introduction	... ...	7
1.	The Saluki – The Living Past	11
2.	Preserving Past Perfection in the Present Day Saluki	19
3.	Judging your Saluki	
	Part One:	31
	Head – Nose – Ears – Teeth – Neck – Chest – Shoulders – Legs – Forelegs – Hindquarters – Loin and Back – Feet – Coat – Colour.	
	Part Two:	46
	Eyes – Paws – Tail – Height – Movement – The Smooth Variety – General Appearance.	
4.	Feeding your Saluki	57
5.	Training and Enjoying your Saluki	65
6.	Coursing your Saluki	77
7.	Imported Salukis	83
Appendix.	The Saluki or Gazelle Hound Club ...	93

Introduction

There have been three objectives in the writing of this book.

FIRSTLY This book will help new owners to understand, appreciate, manage and assess their Salukis. The more people who can apply constructive criticism to any specimen, the better the chance of preserving the essential qualities of any breed. Our national reputation for livestock breeding of all kinds stems from the fact that all sorts and conditions of English men and women in all income groups and all walks of life 'have an eye' for some animal — be it horse, dog, cat, cattle or even budgerigars!

SECONDLY It has seemed important to relate the standard of points as far as possible to the actual conditions pertaining in the *differing areas* of the Middle East which have through the centuries perfected the Saluki as a hunting hound. A standard which lays down a variation of 5 inches in the height of the shoulder must have behind it an appreciation that different sizes of the same basic breed have been perfected for hunting in different conditions of climate and terrain.

A 28" inch Saluki necessary for hunting the wild ass in Persia would be quite unsuitable for stalking a gazelle in the very flat bare country in Iraq described by Mr. Henderson — nor could it comply with the tradition of being carried on the back of an Arab horse of 14.2 hands.

As bitches are proportionately smaller, it follows that a Saluki bitch 21 or 22 inches high at the shoulder must be given an equal chance with larger hounds of being placed in the show ring, provided she is well made in proportion and beautiful in herself.

Very few all-round judges appreciate this point and most have a preconceived idea of what constitutes a correct Saluki size which is only half true. Conversely too few specialist-breed judges really understand the meaning of the word 'sound' and tend to judge too much on preference and prejudice. The very richness of our English language makes for confusion. A sound dog and a sound track have apparently some connection — but only by accident. The sound on the track derives from the Latin *sonare*, to make a noise, while the soundness of the dog stems from Old English *gesund*, meaning healthy, uninjured and therefore *fit for function*. The *varied* function of the Saluki is too little understood and part of the function of this book has been to make it a little more plain.

Surely too the present day function of the Saluki is as a companion to fit into small rooms and small cars!

THIRDLY This book has tried to collect together accurate information on Salukis from many ephemeral sources such as travellers tales, travel books, newspaper and magazine cuttings, letters, and above all the memories of senior Saluki lovers for the benefit of future owners, and Saluki enthusiasts.

Wherever possible, expert Arab opinion has been quoted and recorded before all Arabs become so sophisticated as to forget their ancient hunting skills.

I should like to thank all those owners and breeders who have allowed me to use photographs of their Salukis for this book. In particular I must acknowledge my debt in its preparation to two works: "The Conformation of the Dog" by Mr R.H. Smythe M.R.C.V.S. for the anatomical details, and "The Arab in the Desert" by Colonel H.R.P. Dickinson for its wealth of Arab lore. Lastly and not least I would thank Mrs Pauline Kendall who not only badgered me into writing the book but also undertook the typing!

Vera Watkins

WINDSWIFT SULAYMAN
Head Study by Sally Anne Thompson

Grandson of Taufaan Sharqi (Kuwait breeding) and of Champion Knightellington Caspah. On the distaff side, directly descended from Sabbah through Soraya.

The Saluki drawings used as section-headings through the book were drawn in 1950 by Miss Margaret Baker then aged 13.

The Saluki – The Living Past

1

THE SALUKI — THE LIVING PAST

"I would very much rather give you one of my daughters". The speaker was an Arab, a Sheikh in Iraq honouring the late Mr V.S. Henderson by presenting him with a pair of Salukis. Mr Henderson, who was very happily married, settled for the Salukis! The story illustrates the very special place held by the Saluki in the land of his origin. The presentation to Mr Henderson was a matter of some ceremony. First the Sheikh sent his steward to make sure the Henderson's home was worthy of the Salukis. Later the Sheikh himself with the officers of his household arrived in state to hand over the hounds. The pedigrees of both were recited by a very old tribesman accompanied by his sons. He was the record keeper of the tribe, an hereditary office, and the colour and the hunting abilities of the Salukis' ancestors were given at great length. The recitation could have gone on longer but there was only time for five generations — a total, please note, of 60 hounds remembered in detail and not written down! The Hendersons did that and the pedigree forms were signed by the Sheikh. The bitch incidentally had been brought from the Iran border and was escorted on the journey of around 180 miles by eight fully-armed tribesmen! This was in the early 1950's.

Another anecdote will serve to emphasize the very special place held by the Saluki in comparatively modern Arab life. Some years ago a young man came to buy a Saluki puppy. He had recently returned from the

Middle East where he had been employed as very much a learner in the Pest Control Service. The biblical plagues of ancient Egypt still ravage the area and locusts do enormous damage. Preventative measures include persuading the heads of Arab villages to destroy the locusts while they are still grubs in the ground. This young man, who owned what he admitted to be two very indifferent Salukis, was accompanying his superior officer who was owned by a really magnificent Red Setter. But the learner boy had to do all the talking whenever they came to an Arab village. He owned Salukis and was therefore listened to because his rank must be much higher than that of the man who merely owned a Kelb — i.e. Red Setter. His Salukis gained the boy a hearing. The expert senior officer could get nowhere!

And so — what is a Saluki? Why is it so special? The classic description reads as follows:—
Essentially the Saluki is a sporting dog, a capable hound of the chase with his sloping shoulders, racy hindquarters, flexible loin, deep ribs, long stretching limbs and muscular neck. He is admirably adapted for the work for which he has been bred for so many centuries — the hunting of Gazelle and Hares in the Desert as meat supply for his Master — the Bedouin Arab. He is fashioned for speed, quick turning, running on rough ground and for endurance. Elegant in shape and graceful in movement, points of special Saluki beauty are their beautiful proportions, finely moulded heads and muzzles, their arched necks and sinuous lines, their bright humanly expressive eyes and the silky feathering of their drooping ears and long curved tails. In size they may vary from 23-28 inches at the shoulder with bitches proportionately smaller. In some districts they are carried on the Arab horse to keep them fresh for the chase when game is sighted. By tradition they are not bought or sold but presented as marks of honour from one potentate to another. The genuine breed is found on all the ancient trade routes throughout Arabia, Syria, Mesopotamia, Persia, Egypt, and Northern Africa.

It is easy to wax lyrical over the romance of the Saluki — but this is not enough. The Saluki, in addition to being a normal naughty lovable dog, is in himself a work of art perfected over many thousands of years for doing a vital job — supplying his master with food. As such he presents us with a challenge: to keep that perfection of centuries unimpaired, despite the changes modern civilisation is bringing to those areas of the ancient world which produced him.

Of course, changes wrought by modern conditions are not confined to the Middle East. Apart from the geographical extent, this also affects

The Living Past 15

the world of dogs. Comparatively few of the 100 odd breeds exhibited at Cruft's — the most famous Dog Show in the world — look exactly the same today as they did at the first Cruft's show in 1886. Afghans seem to have lost the traditional saddle of short hair, while some breeds like the Doberman Pinscher have actually been invented since Cruft's started. Man's instinct to adopt, adapt and improve is strong, but the process applied to works of art is usually disastrous.

So it is with the Saluki and our responsibility is one of conservation, constant watchfulness to ensure that essential characteristics of this lovely breed are preserved and passed on to future generations, as they have been so carefully guarded for the last 5,000 years. "Are these not the inheritance of our fathers and shall we not to our sons bequeath them?"

Many civilisations and cultures have risen, flourished and declined, and vanished in the vast area we call the Middle East which is larger than all Europe — and is also the cradle of the three most influential Religions in the World today: the Jewish, the Christian and the Muslim, to put them in chronological order.

Civilisation, old or new, implies the existence of a people sufficiently prosperous to have made convenient arrangements for the supply of their essential bodily needs, such as shelter, food, clothing, so as to have sufficient leisure to exercise their minds in the realms of craftsmanship, literature, pictorial art, Music and architecture, etc.

The treasures of Tutankhamen are a case in point. The finds of archaeologists — rare manuscripts, great paintings, even folklore and travellers tales — all leave clues as to what life was like in past ages. This in fact is where we find evidence of the importance and value attached to the Saluki. This is how we know that he has been bred as the Companion of Kings for around 5,000 years. This is how we know that his breeding has been kept pure for all these centuries — so set apart from ordinary dogs that the very language of his peoples has a special word for him: *Tazi* in Persian, *Saluki* in Arabic where the word for ordinary dog is *Kelb*. The evidence for this is even deeper still. Even today, dogs of other breeds take very little notice of a Saluki bitch "in season" and many Salukis (but not all!) just will not mate with a dog of another breed.

The well-known archaeologist Professor Selwyn Lloyd excavating in Iraq around 1948, discovered what must have been a fabulous avenue of 200 temple tombs at Tel Abu. In one of them was found the perfectly preserved skeleton of a hound — almost certainly that of a Saluki — laid across the body of a 15-year old boy. From calculations made it would appear that these 200 tombs were already an ancient monument and probably forgotten *before* Abraham left Ur of the Chaldees as recorded in the book of Genesis. We know from Egyptian sources that he reached

Egypt, after many years of wandering, around 2081 B.C.

There are in fact even older traces of Saluki representation in the art of ancient civilisation. Coming nearer to our own day, Persian poetry and Persian miniature paintings have many references to the Saluki apart from those which Arab scholars have brought to our notice.

Salukis nearly always come into notice in Europe after wars. This was specially so at the time of the Crusades, when a Saluki at home was proof that a Knight had indeed been to the Holy Land. It was so after World War I, when the Sarona strain and the El Nablous kennels were established, and again after World War II.

From the foregoing it will be realised that Salukis (they were sometimes known as Persian Greyhounds) are almost certainly the oldest variety extant of the Greyhound family — King Solomon's Greyhound in fact. They have enjoyed, and kept the privilege of being, not only noble "El-Hor", but also the nobility's hounds. In the Middle Ages, in England it was an offence under the Forest Laws for an ordinary individual to own a greyhound. Such ownership had to have a warrant from the King and was not lightly given. Even so, Salukis in the Middle East have kept their ranks as Royal Dogs. The best, as we have seen, even today are not bought and sold among the Arabs but only presented as marks of honour. This status, allied to their obvious beauty, has caught the imagination of many artists through the centuries. A particularly interesting painting of "Two Hounds" is in the FOGG Museum of Art at Harvard University. It is dated 1452 A.D. and attributed to Tsuan-Te. They are obviously Salukis — one of them wears a jewelled collar and the painting is interesting evidence that Salukis were in China in the 15th Century. There are in fact pictures of Salukis in China being carried in front of the riders on horses dating from 10th century and even earlier: presents no doubt from King to King down the great Silk Road, perhaps the oldest trading route in the world. Many artists in Europe in the 16th, 17th & 18th centuries used Salukis in their pictures as a mark of Royalty. Paul Veronese frequently did so, as did Bassano and Tiepolo. A particularly striking example is shown in our reproduction of Tintoretto's painting (now in Toronto) of Christ washing the feet of the Disciples. The mark of Royalty, the Saluki is in the foreground facing towards Christ and has another function as well. Blot it out with a piece of dark paper and you will see three separate pictures of three groups; take the paper away and you will have one picture again! Chasing Salukis around art galleries at home or abroad can be absorbing interest for any holiday, as well as improving one's cultural outlook generally! Keen Saluki seekers can find one in the stained glass windows of the Vestry in the 14th Century Parish Church of St. Mary at Warwick. You

TINTORETTO (Jacopo Robusti); Italian, 1518-1594 – *Christ Washing His Disciples' Feet* (detail), early 1550s oil on canvas 61" x 160½". ART GALLERY OF ONTARIO, Toronto. Gift by General Subscription, 1959

The Saluki is a traditional sign of Royalty. Note the resemblance to Sabbah the Windswift on page 27 may have to ask the Verger to show it to you as Vestries are usually locked! In the 18th Century, English art began to associate Salukis with the Arab Horse (a subject developed later). Among the modern Artists we must count Sir Alfred Munnings, and when it comes to Art in Photography, the work of Miss Sally Anne Thompson must not be forgotten.

Last but not least, mention must be made of the bas-relief in bronze made by Benevenuto Cellini in 1544 for the Grand Duke Cosmo de Medici. The original is now in the National Museum in Florence, but members of the Saluki Club can see an excellent replica at least once a year at the Saluki Club Open Show in England. This was given by the Honourable Florence Amherst to the Saluki Club as an annual award for the best imported Saluki as an undoubted mark of her conviction that to keep a Saluki in its perfection we must from time to time go back to the land of its origin.

2

Preserving the Saluki

2

PRESERVING PAST PERFECTION IN THE PRESENT DAY SALUKI

Heredity, despite advanced learning on genes and mutations, remains a very strange and mysterious thing.

In the early 1930's I had the privilege of knowing an old lady aged about 85. She was unquestionably also a great lady despite the fact that she lived, very proudly and graciously, in *one* room on £1.00 per week (10/- old age pension and 10/- from some benevolent trust). She was the living image of portraits of King Louis 14th of France! She was in fact descended from a Maid of Honour who had accompanied to France Minette, sister of Charles II, when she married the Duke of Orleans — brother of the King. The Sun King had a very roving eye and though this old lady's family, in an excess of Victorian respectability had melted down the elegant piece of plate presented to mark the royal liaison, it was established over more than 200 years that one member of each generation bore this striking resemblance to the old King. *One* member be it noted. Consider the number of generations in 200 years and the size of families particularly in Victorian days (my father was the 17th out of a family of 20) and there must be many descendants who do *not* bear this striking resemblance and who in fact look different, and so it is with dogs. A Swedish breeder of Salukis saw a photograph of Windswift Soraya. He said at once, "Find me a Saluki like that and I'll buy it". I explained that though she was now an ancestor of my whole kennel, I myself was still trying to breed (or find) her like. Of the dozens of Salukis bred by me and seen by me, none have been quite like her — all were different and most have passed on their differences. This is important. Salukis of the past do turn up in the present and will turn up in the future, but often at intervals of many years and people who are new to the breed do not recognise them for their essential good qualities.

It is in fact very very difficult to keep any breed of dog at its perfect best. This indeed is the ultimate object of all Dog Shows and most sports involving dogs. With Salukis it is particularly difficult for many reasons.

The art of many civilisations shows us the Saluki as part of the way of life of great nobles and Kings throughout ancient and comparatively modern history. In nearly every case they are recognisable as Salukis, but in the art idiom of the day. The artist was only concerned with his central theme of recording an historical occasion or honouring (and flattering) his patron potentate. He was not recording the Saluki in detail as a hound of interest to posterity. Probably it would never occur to him that a Saluki could change. He was part of life — catching meat for his masters. He was the best of his race obtainable and any hound failing to live up to the very high standards demanded by those masters would be ruthlessly destroyed. We know from several sources that even now litters of Salukis born in the Desert are most drastically culled by their Arab owners — partly of course because life is hard and food is scarce for man and beast, so only the best deserves to be fed. There is also the question of prestige: no Bedouin Chief of any consequence will keep an animal, hound, hawk or horse which could fairly be criticised adversely by his fellow Sheikhs.

By contrast, very few people who breed dogs in England, either regularly or just once from a pet bitch, ever dream of putting down puppies even when these are obviously far from perfect specimens. Inevitably therefore in every breed there are many imperfect dogs and bitches in circulation. So needs change. The American Cocker has "evolved" from the English Cocker Spaniel. The average Afghan would find hunting in his country of origin very difficult with his present day heavy coat and the Shetland Sheepdog has been invented within the present century.

But with the Saluki as already mentioned we are dealing with a work of art perfected over 5,000 years and the problem is one of conservation. The danger is very real that unless we are careful we shall end up — doubtless with a nice dog — but it won't be a Saluki!

So what is the perfect Saluki like? Where do we go for the knowledge with which to judge them, either in the Show Ring or at home?

The obvious answer is the Bedouin Arab. But he is changing too and tracking down his traditional hound-lore and inherited expert opinion is not as easy as it might seem. The Bedouin Chieftain is not readily accessible even to visitors who speak Arabic. He keeps no written records and the circumstances of Desert life are changing very rapidly. Before there were guns, the Bedouin Arab's only hope of any meat was what the Saluki caught for him. In certain parts it is so still. But oil has brought great wealth to many of the leading families of the area and the traditional necessity of carrying a Saluki on the back of an Arab horse or on camel back in order to keep him fresh for the chase when a herd of gazelle might be sighted, is no longer necessary. Salukis are taken today in Cadillacs and the slaughter of gazelles with guns has reached such proportions that many Arab governments have forbidden the sport in the interest of preserving the gazelles from total extinction. Moreover it is important to remember that by no means all Arabs are interested in Salukis. The Sheiks and princes are largely inaccesible in their still feudal way of life. The younger sophisticates have little or no use for the traditional hound-knowledge and horsemanship which we admire so much.

At the first Open Show of the Saluki Club held with the Arab Horse Society's Show at Roehampton in 1954, the Anglo Arab Association held a garden party on the ground. The late Mr Brian Chambers, a very knowledgeable Saluki judge, made a point of talking to as many as possible of the Arabs present to find out what they thought of English Salukis. Very few were interested and fewer still had any real knowledge. On a later occasion when a demonstration of Arab hunting with Hawk and Saluki was planned, it was quite difficult to find among the Arab Embassies in London any Arab capable of riding an Arab horse despite the fact that H.M. the Queen was expected to visit the show! Of course Arab experts on the Saluki do exist. I have had the privilege of meeting some and it's a real education to watch them going over the hounds. But they are few and hard to find. Next to the traditional Arab owner-breeder our most fruitful source of information is likely to be those explorers and travellers in the Middle East who recorded their experiences in the days when the area was largely unknown. Or those Service personnel both civil and military who have had occasion to act as advisors on various matters to the many Sheikhs and Emirs of the Arabian East. For the most part these were (and are) people who by their upbringing have a natural 'eye' for horses and hounds, a real interest in various forms of hunting, and the educational ability to write about it.

It has already been mentioned that Salukis tend to come into prominence after wars and it was after World War I, when serving in Syria, that Brigadier General Lance was given a pair of Salukis. One of those was the well known Dog Champion Sarona Kelb. On their return to England, General and Mrs Lance set about getting Salukis recognised by the Kennel Club as an individual breed. This was in 1922 and 1923 and the interest aroused was newsworthy. A large number of magazines and periodicals published articles on the Saluki and in nearly every case authors were people of authority on various parts of the Middle East where Salukis were to be found and they were writing from personal experience.

But though general interest in Salukis was thus stimulated in the early 1920's, General Lance was by no means the first or only enthusiast to bring specimens of the breed to England. There had been one or two "Persian Greyhounds" listed among foreign dogs in the Kennel Club Stud Book and Calendar from 1874 onwards. The earliest true enthusiast for the breed was the Honourable Florence Amherst, daughter of Lord Amherst of Hackney, to whom a pair of Salukis was given by Mr. W. Jennings Bramley in 1895. Miss Amherst was one of those people to whom the 19th Century term 'orientalist' might well be applied. She had travelled extensively probably with her father who was interested in Egyptian antiques. She counted amoung her friends many prominent persons in Arabia and other Eastern countries. As early as 1907 she wrote an authoritative pamphlet on the breed. She was the first President of the Saluki Club which was founded in 1923. Her Saluki prefix was *Amherstia*. Miss Joan Mitchell was another Saluki enthusiast who spent 15 years in Palestine as a nurse and was finally Matron of Nablous Hospital. Her el Nablous Kennel was founded there and a pair, *Ebni* and *Binte* El Nablous, came with her to England on her retirement. They were a brother and sister sired by Jack of Jerusalem, a Saluki very well thought of in the area belonging to a Palestine breeder from whom Miss Amherst also imported several Salukis. There were in addition several other people in England who had been honoured in the traditional way by various Sheikhs and Emirs with the gift of one or a pair of Salukis.

All these people were enthusiasts and Saluki lovers, but all were puzzled to find that like the stars in St Paul's immortal phrase "one Saluki differed from another in glory", and because each Saluki had been presented as a genuine mark of honour, each owner was convinced that his or her Saluki was "the right type"!

The controversy raged between the wars, was still going strong when I knew General Lance and Miss Mitchell in 1948/1956, and is not wholly resolved now.

The urgent matter at the time however (1922/23), in the interests of the breed, was to form a Club and draw up a standard of points which the Kennel Club could adopt and approve. Despite much argument, it was

Above: The Honourable Florence Amherst, who introduced Saluki to Britain in 1897 with Champion Zobeid and his litter brother Farhan bred from South Arabian imports. (Photograph by Thomas Fall.)

Below: The author with two English Salukis, descendants of Sabbah, purchased by an Arab expert on behalf of the ruler of a southern Sheikhdom. The taller, the bitch, was 24 inches at the shoulder. (Photograph by Kent & Sussex Courier)

done, and it was very cleverly done to include all the types then in Britain!

Discussion of detail follows later, but one item will make the point. Under Height, the standard reads "from 23 to 28 inches at the shoulder with bitches proportionately smaller" — a variation of 5 inches or more in the same breed of hound!

Some people may well ask what is a standard of points? It is in fact a sort of blueprint for the breed, setting out in detail what is required for a dog to be a good specimen. It is not often realised that, quite apart from the question of height mentioned above, several individual dogs can conform to the standard point by point and yet not look alike, but they will have the necessary attributes for which the breed was developed. A touching human incident will illustrate the point. It is on record that a girl aged around 18-20 who had been born blind, was suddenly by some miracle of surgery or natural causes enabled to see. She was asked by a journalist what impressed her most about the seen world. She replied "everybody's faces are so different". Hitherto she had learnt people's faces by touch, and everybody had nose, eyes, chin, cheeks, lips, etc. (in fact a standard of points) yet they all felt very much alike. Vision found them differing from each other considerably. This is a fact, of course, which most of us take for granted regarding the human face, but often fail to see the parallel when it comes to dogs!

More than fifty years have now passed since the formation of the Saluki Club and the production by the officers of that club of the first standard of points for the breed, and that agreed standard covered several variations in what was obviously one very beautiful race of hounds.

Moreover it must be remembered not only that all these Saluki enthusiasts were people with first hand knowledge of the breed in its countries of origin, but also that the various Saluki types about which they argued are still with us. Those Salukis were mated with each other. Sarona to Amherstia, Amherstia to El Nablous, El Nablous to Sarona, and so on. The first declared object of the club was "to promote the breeding of Salukis by endeavouring to make the qualities of the breed better known". As they were promoting the breed, the puppies were not culled nor was perfection clearly defined. In one way this was a continuation of an age-long Saluki tradition. To this day, Salukis are not bought or sold in Arab lands. They have always been presented as marks of honour from one king or Chieftain to another, and must have been exchanged all over the travel and trade routes of the ancient world. Thus each noble Lord from time to time had fresh blood introduced into his own strain of Saluki. Miss Amherst herself gives authoritative evidence for this, and for the variation in type, in an article on the breed published in Hutchinson's Dog Encyclo-

Above: Sabbah the Windswift, a Royal gift from Saudi Arabia, and in Arab eyes a good Saluki. 28 English Champions (of the 64 made up since his arrival) carry his blood. (Photograph by Thomas Fall)

Below: Windswift Soraya, daughter of Sabbah the Windswift, ex Windswift Yasmin. (Photograph by Thomas Fall)

paedia which is now out of print. "There are many varieties and variations of the breed which form a most interesting study. The principal divisions into which the Arabs class Salukis are the 'feathered' called *Shami* (Syrian) and the 'smooth' called *Nejdi* (from Nejd).

In Persia, the Saluki, having been for centuries valued for the chase by people of distinction, came to be known (especially the feathered variety) as the Persian Greyhound. The Persians called it the *Tazi* or Arabian (as the Arab is termed by the Persian) denoting their Arabian origin. These Salukis became larger and heavier with longer hair, and breeders renew their stock from the south." Elsewhere in the same article we are told "in the East the colour of hounds is selected by the tribes to suit the districts over which they have to hunt their quarry". In view of this, the problem of black and tan Salukis puzzled the writer for a long time. The answer came one morning in the London Times describing how Syrian planes had buzzed H.M. King Hussein of Jordan piloting himself, "the planes wheeled and dived over the black lava Desert". Black Desert, black Salukis, so obviously red-gold Desert, red-gold Salukis etc. To sum up, apart from Miss Amherst and her very scholarly account based on travel and first hand accounts from explorers and administrators, we have the evidence of Miss Joan Mitchell and the hounds she introduced after spending 15 years in a country of their origin. We have General Lance, a cavalryman and serving soldier (and a keen naturalist), commanding troops in Syria in war time. We have an account of hunting with the Saluki in an article "the new Sporting Magazine dated September, 1837", and another by J. Wentworth Day in the 1930's. Colonel H.R.P. Dickson in his exhaustive study "The Arab in the Desert" published in 1949, gives valuable information on the modern Desert Saluki. We have the testimony already referred to of the late Mr. Victor Henderson and Mrs. Henderson, besides the witness of several recently imported hounds. One of these in particular is worthy of a mention.

In 1950 that remarkable Arab personality H.M. King Abdul Aziz ibn Saud of Saudi Arabia presented a Saluki as a traditional mark of honour to his Ambassador in London His Excellency Shaikh Hafiz Wahaba M.R.V.O. King ibn Saud would not have become the most prominent and powerful Arab Statesman-Ruler of his day if he had not been remarkably shrewd and politically astute. We also know from the author of "Arabian Jubilee" that the King, regarding himself as the father-figure of his people, had habitually a remarkable memory and concern for detail. It is inconceivable that such a ruler would risk his prestige in one of the World's leading capitals by allowing anything but the very best and most typical hound to be sent as a gift. The Saluki in question *Sabbah* (The Morning) was in fact bred by the King's own nephew the Amir Mohammed ibn Saud. This Saluki was later presented to the writer by the Ambassador, as Embassy life clearly did not suit him! His importance to the breed lies in the fact that he represented as late as 1950 what the then leading Arab Ruler, himself a keen hunter, regarded as a really good Saluki — and at a time when from Abraham to ibn Saud for a period of nearly 4,000 years, the ways of the Desert had altered so little that the patriarchs might have well have felt at home.

Of 64 English Champions made up since 1953, no less than 29 carry Sabbah's blood, besides many American, Scandinavian and other European Champions.

3

Judging your Saluki

3

JUDGING YOUR SALUKI

Part One:

A Khalif once sent his servant to buy him a horse. But the servant fearing the price of failure was reluctant to go and said he knew nothing about horses. To which the Khalif replied "You know a well-bred Saluki and the points which govern speed and endurance. Look for these points in the horse."

Another quotation describes the Saluki as "the hound built like a horse".

The Arab may well be said to have perfected the horse for transport and war, and the Saluki for supplying him with food, for both speed and endurance are essential. Certainly there are many points of similarity between the Arab horse and the Arab hound. Both have refined heads (some Salukis have dish faces like an Arab horse) and elegant long necks. The sloping shoulders and good spring of rib, with deep strong chests, width between the hip bones, the long strong quarters, and particularly the movement are also very alike. Most people with an eye for a good horse can pick out a good Saluki. But the average Saluki owner probably never wants to own a horse.

Nevertheless, whatever you plan for your Saluki, whether to show him, to course him or just to enjoy him, there is a lot of satisfaction in knowing how to assess him. It's specially useful too when buying a puppy to be able to assess that puppy's parents and so make a guess at his future potential.

As mentioned in the previous chapter, over fifty years ago the committee of the newly formed Saluki or Gazelle Hound Club drew up a standard of points for the Breed which in fact covered the variety of Saluki types owned by the then members of the Club, most of whom had acquired their hounds as gifts in the Middle East and had personal experience of their desert habitat.

Today very few Saluki owners and still fewer Saluki judges have any knowledge of those desert conditions in which the Saluki was bred to hunt. Also, though most judges worth their salt do study the standard of points before judging the breed, the new Saluki owner or exhibitor may find it hard to understand. In January 1970, the Committee of the Saluki Club, of which the writer was a member, produced an interpretation of the standard with notes for breeders and judges. This forms the basis for the following explanations with reference where necessary to what we know of knowledgeable Arab requirements in the breed.

Over the years a good deal of controversy has arisen over certain points. So for ease of reference, the *order* of the Standard of Points has been altered and the controversial clauses are discussed in Part Two of this Chapter.

The words of the standard issued by the Kennel Club are set in italics.

HEAD   *"Long and narrow, skull moderately wide between the ears, not domed, stop not pronounced, the whole showing great quality."*

The first six words look like a contradiction in terms until it is realised that "Skull moderately wide between the ears" is a safeguard against a Borzoi type head which in a Saluki would be too narrow. There must be room for a Saluki's brains! "Stop not pronounced" does not mean no stop at all, but the slope must be very gradual. The standard in fact allows for two shapes of head: one is obviously a long triangle, the other is shorter and much more the shape of a fox-head. Both are correct provided the head shows great refinement, is not domed on top and is not coarse, clumsy or heavy. Some Salukis with very good heads appear (as aforementioned) slightly dish-faced like an Arab horse.

NOSE *"Black or Liver".*

This is a point where prejudice sometimes affects judging in the show ring. Some Salukis have a reddish-brown nose, not pink like under-cooked livers (!) but brown, and this is quite correct. It should not of course be patchy, though some puppies start out with patchy noses and they grow to solid colour. Champion Bedouin Caliph owned by Miss Deborah Steeds (now Mrs. Copperthwaite) has a liver nose and has won 24 Challenge Certificates under 24 different judges and this is a record for the breed — at present!

EARS *"Long and covered with long silky hair hanging close to the skull and mobile".*

The leather of the ear, i.e. the ear itself, should be long enough for the bottom tip to reach the corner of the mouth when brought forward (not pulled). The actual length of the "long silky hair" can and does vary according both to the breeding and the state of the coat. Some Salukis, especially black ones, have very long ear feathering hanging up to 5 inches and more below the tip of the leathers. In others the silky hair seems to sprout only from the top of the ear and never grows to hang down much below the leather. It is however still long and silky compared to the short hair on the body and conforms to the standard.

A correspondent writing about his Salukis in the desert some 60 years ago, writes of his 10 Salukis, mostly from Mesopotamia: "When running in scrub country, heavy feather collected plant burrs, so was to that extent a nuisance, but I did not notice that it ordinarily affected either speed or stamina." "Mobile" is an important test of temperament about which the standard says nothing elsewhere. A specialist Saluki judge has placed a dog largely because "he used his ears" and the well known Mr R.H. Smythe, M.R.C.V.S., states in an article on ears: "Ears in certain breeds should reflect the intelligence of the dog and the interest it takes in its surroundings. No doubt ears play their part too in canine conversation." A Saluki who never voluntarily moves its ears in the show ring can be almost too terrified to move at all! As with a horse, the movement of the ears can be a sign of the thinking going on between them.

TEETH *"Strong and Level"*

Teeth can be either edge to edge or with a good scissor bite where the bottom teeth come very very close in behind the upper teeth. Mouths are very important for the catching and holding of game.

A bad mouth is a very serious fault, particularly in a hunting hound, and one that is hereditary. But it doesn't affect a Saluki's lovable character. If yours (male or female) has a bad mouth, i.e. where the top teeth are far in advance of the bottom or vice versa, he or she will still do well in his major role as an honoured companion, but should not be bred from.

It sometimes happens that a puppy grows his top jaw faster than his bottom jaw which later catches up. In this case he will be all right for showing but the question of breeding from that puppy should, for the sake of the breed as a whole, be considered only in exceptional circumstances.

NECK   *"Long supple and well muscled".*

Despite the muscle, the neck must not look thick. There are only seven bones in any dog's neck be he Pekingese or Irish Wolfhound — these are the cervical vertebrae of the spine. These vertebrae not only vary in size according to the breed of the dog, but they can vary in length between dogs of the same breed. They also vary in length between different parts of the same dog — cervical, dorsal, lumbar etc.

A good Saluki needs long neck bones and long dorsal bones. A long well muscled neck is important for speed and balance and for picking up game. Of course one end of the neck carries the head and the other is set into the shoulder and, to quote Mr. R.H. Smythe again: "Necks and shoulders run in pairs", and long necks and good shoulders often go together. The long neck should fit into the shoulder, not at a right-angle but gracefully, as though the two parts had been sculptured. The muscle of the neck is very important because the Saluki works at speed. In some parts of the Middle East, the Saluki brings down his Gazelle by diving under the leaping deer and catching its throat from beneath. This, at speed, demands tremendous strength. New owners of Salukis should take special care never to let their pet pull away from them backwards in his collar. It can happen when a young dog panics suddenly in traffic, or it can happen if a Saluki is left tied up when he has not been trained to know that that means he must 'stay'. They can flex those neck muscles out so much that the neck becomes wider than the head and the collar is slipped. In emergency, grab your Saluki by any part of his anatomy but don't rely on the collar! A slip lead or choke chain is safer in one way but throttling an already scared dog makes the panic worse, and when he's at ease in a slip lead he is quite clever enough to know when your mind is else-where, put down his head for a seemingly ordinary sniff when slack and off goes the lead, off and fast goes the hound. But of course he will always come home!

The carriage of the head and neck is also important. There is a long neck muscle stretching down from the base of the skull. At its lower end, parts are attached to each humerus or arm bone, i.e. the bone joining the point of the shoulder to the elbow under the brisket. The contraction of this muscle pulls up the arm, and with it the knee and foot, and so helps to advance the limb to its utmost at every stride. This muscle can only work with full efficiency when the neck is fully outstretched and the head held high.

CHEST *"Deep and moderately narrow".*

This is very important and the first thing an Arab looks for in a Saluki. He wants it deep and strong! There are three view points for judging the chest: (i) The front, (ii) the side, (iii) the top, looking down on the hound.

Seen from the side, the curved brisket of the Saluki should almost, if not quite, touch the point of the elbow. Strategic brushing up the elbow feathering can help the looks but won't deceive a good judge who may well ask the dog's age. Salukis are not fully developed until between three and four years old, and full depth may not develop until then. Seen from the front, it should appear well defined and strong like a horse's chest or as though there were a breast plate under the skin. Too often the front legs seem to finish in an inverted 'V' and the whole hound at this point appears weak and too narrow for good heartroom!

On the other hand, heaviness here is to be deplored. The standard clearly states "moderately narrow"! Exaggerated breadth whether or not accompanied by 'loaded' or over-muscled shoulders can make a Saluki 'front heavy' and affect vital balance at full speed.

We talk of heartroom in our hounds when what we really mean is lung room — room for the lungs to expand and contract. Next to the seven vertebrae in the neck come the 18 dorsal vertebrae of the spine, and 18 pairs of curved ribs fit into the spaces between the vertebrae. Thirteen of these form the chest cavity which houses heart and lungs and the major blood vessels.

As breath is drawn in, the curved ribs rotate upon their own axes and enlarge the chest laterally. Because there is always a potential vacuum behind the surface of the lungs and the lining of the chest wall, the lungs are compelled to follow the movement of the ribs and to fill up with air as the volume of the chest increases. This means too that the relative space between each pair of ribs is also important. So the longer these 18 dorsal vertebrae are, the greater the space between the ribs and the more room the lungs have to expand as they fill with air. This is why 'spring of rib' is important to a Saluki. He should not be barrel-shaped, but neither should his depth of brisket be 'slab sided'. Seen from above, there should be a definite curving out of the ribs behind the withers or point of the shoulder and in front of the loin.

SHOULDERS *"Shoulders sloping and set well back; well-muscled without being coarse".*

The standard heads this point "Forequarters but shoulders are so important that the specific heading is justified." By shoulder is meant the flat shoulder blade or scapula, which at its lower and narrower end is joined to the top of the humerus or upper arm at the point of the dog's chest. The upper or broad end of the scapula is attached by muscles to the dorsal vertebrae or back bones (the 2nd to the 7th) and also to the ribs. Like those in the neck, these dorsal bones can be long or short. When these and those of the neck are long not only, as already explained, is there more room for lung expansion but also the top of the shoulder must be attached further back towards the tail of the dog, so that it lies at an oblique angle between the point of the dog's chest and what in a horse is known as the withers on the top of his back. This is what is known as a shoulder "well laid back" and the term can be muddling. The shoulder blade is tilted backwards on its edge and *not* — looking from the side — laid back away from you as if you were opening the lid of a box!

In an upright or straight shoulder, the shoulder blade which you can feel and see under the skin when the dog is moving in a good light, goes almost vertically upwards towards the base of the neck (which will then probably be short) and makes a very small angle in relation to the ground instead of near 45%, i.e. half of a right-angle as it should in a Saluki.

There are two important reasons for valuing a "well set back" or sloping shoulder in a Saluki. One is a lessening of concussion, the shock of landing when travelling at speed over hard and often rocky ground. The shock with each stride travels to the spine more or less directly from the ground if pasterns as well as shoulders are upright and can damage the bones through which it passes. But a sloping pastern and sloping shoulder mean a series of shock absorbing springs or changes of route between ground and spine which lessens the impact and makes for less wear and tear on bones, ligaments, and the nerves in the spinal cord.

More important is a question of *reach.* The humerus and with it the front leg and paw cannot move further forward than into a straight line with the scapular or shoulder blade. Produce a line through the centre of a straight or upright shoulder and it meets the ground well behind a similar line drawn through a sloping or oblique shoulder blade. A sloping shoulder can thus add several inches to each forward stride of the hound and

Judging Your Saluki

increase the speed accordingly.
   One more important factor of shoulder placement must be emphasised. The top of each shoulder blade ends in a semi-circular piece of cartilage. These come together as the dog puts its head down (to pick up game). It is essential that there should be sufficient clearance (in the Saluki about 2 fingers width) between these cartilages or withers when the dog is standing normally. Some judges will pull a dog's head gently to the ground with one hand while the fingers of the other are testing the closure at the withers. Too much galloping too young, or puppies continually jumping up at the door of a pen, can develop too much muscle under the shoulder blades and this can act as a wedge to keep the shoulder blades apart. When this happens the muscles outside the shoulder may well be overdeveloped too and the clean line of the shoulder and front is spoilt.

LEGS   A good Saluki when fully adult has very strong legs. General Lance told the writer that once, when he was out walking with his hounds running loose, two of them jumped over the wall of a railway bridge on to the rack of a deep cutting below. He said "I raced down to the line dreading what I should find. But the Salukis had picked themselves up with a shake and gone serenely on their way." Nevertheless, young Salukis — i.e. under 2 years old — should not be encouraged to jump hedges or walls where landing means a long drop on to a hard road.

FORELEGS   *"Straight and long from the elbow to the knee".*

The length of the front legs should of course be proportionate to the size of the Saluki, remembering that there can be a variation of five inches in the height at the top of the shoulders.
   Straight front legs are very important and a lot depends on the Saluki's upbringing.
   In a normal puppy at least up to 9 months old (and probably much later in a Saluki which is a late developing breed) all the long bones — the two in the front leg, and the thigh and shin in the hind leg — consist really of three parts: a central shaft which forms the length of the bone and a thickened portion at each end which carries the joint surface. As the puppy grows, the shaft lengthens while the end pieces stay put. During puppy-hood these ends are united to the shaft by cartilage or gristle only and it is comparatively soft and pliable. This means of course that the ends are movable. Often it is only when the dog is fully grown that enough particles of lime have settled in the gristle to build it into bone so that the fully-developed shaft and the two ends become converted into one solid structure.

This is why young puppies should have enough space to grow and play contentedly, and not spend their time jumping up and down on a concrete floor and scrabbling at the door of a kennel. This can throw the end pieces out of line with the main shaft and cause eventual if slight deformity. In extreme cases the shaft bone itself can become bent if feeding and *walking* exercise are either deficient, or, in some cases, excessive.

A tired puppy must rest *at once* and never be asked to walk home on weary legs!

A very important point to remember is that bones vary in quality. Heavy bone is *not* synonymous with best quality. It is *density* and not thickness of bone which matters. Here the analogy with the horse so often associated with the Saluki can help and probably largely explain, the early controversy on Saluki type. Lt Colonel Sidney Gold-Schmidt's book "An eye for a Horse" states under bone: "The texture of bone, as revealed by post-mortem examination, varies from an ivory-like density to a consistency more of the nature of pumice-stone. The former is found in the highest degree of perfection in the high-class Arab under 15 hands bred and reared in the desert on hard dry food. The latter is typified by the large Shire horse bred and reared in the marshy fens and fed on grass. Taking 15.3 as the average height of the modern Thoroughbred horse reared under civilised conditions, the bigger we breed him above the standard, the more porous will be the texture of the bones and the more liable to exosmosis and kindred diseases."

That well-known judge Miss Enid Nicholls who comes from a family famed for their knowledge and experience of all types of dogs was going over Sabbah the Windswift from Saudi Arabia. He had plenty of substance but very fine bone. As she felt his foreleg, she turned to me saying "You are a lucky woman."

There are two other points in the Arab judging of Salukis which deserves our attention in connection with forelegs. *Elbows should be difficult to press together.* This is not meant to try the strength of a judge's vice-like grip! The idea is to test springiness, development, and strength of the pectoral muscles which brace the elbows to the sides of the chest. When these pectoral muscles are soft and flabby, the elbow appears slack and the dog will be out of elbows. When they are firm, well developed and contracting normally the elbows are drawn in tightly to the sides and do not 'wobble' as the dog comes towards you.

Wrists should be small — this is self explanatory.

Judging Your Saluki 41

HINDQUARTERS *"Strong, hipbones set wide apart and stifle moderately bent, hocks low to the ground showing galloping and jumping power."*

The Arabs want 3 of 4 (man's) fingers width between the two hip bones on the top of the back: a deep hollow between the bones is thought to be very good.

The hip bones are to the pelvis very much what the withers are to the scapular, and in each case there must be room between them. The pelvis is firmly attached to the sacrum or end vertebrae of the spine (between the lumbar vertebrae and the tail bones) by ligaments which allow little or no movement between the two. It consists of three bones fused together to form a long girdle containing a central orifice by means of which the inside of the body communicates with the outside world. It ends up with the two seat bones just below the tail. In the Saluki the pelvis should be long and sloping at an angle with the ground at about $30°$ — $35°$. Occasionally one sees a Saluki whose rear end seems to have been squared off sharply. This must mean either that the pelvis is shorter than it should be (and in a bitch this will mean a smaller orifice and difficult whelping) or that for some reason the pelvis is set on more or less vertically, which would affect speed and movement very badly

Attached to the pelvis is the femur or thigh above the stifle joint — then comes the tibia and fibular and then the hock. The hind leg ends with the bones of the pasterns and foot.

As the dog moves, the foot pushes against the ground and the unyielding ground passes the impulse back to the limb through the hock, tibia, femur and pelvis, and then through its unyielding joint with the sacrum straight along the spine. So the dog moves forward. If the pelvis is too vertical, the impulse instead of going forward would tend to push the lower part of the pelvis upwards against the back bone and the forward movement would be impaired if not lost. The Saluki being a sight hound must always be ready to "take-off" at speed after game. His starting power depends on his ability to push his feet against the ground on the instant by straightening his hind legs from bends and angles to complete extension both forcibly and rapidly. So he needs a moderate bend of stifle (over angulation would take too long to straighten) always more or less 'at the ready', and to operate the whole propelling force he needs tremendous muscle power in a well-developed second thigh. This muscle should be large and strong. You can feel it in the front part of the upper leg bone or femur underneath the coat.

Many owners in the show ring hide this valuable bend of stifle by stretching their Saluki's legs right out behind it as though they were showing a Whippet. (Possibly through some idea of "covering the ground"!) But this creates the fault "straight stifle" when probably it isn't there at all! This point should be considered by those enthusiasts who prefer to track race their Salukis as distinct from coursing them naturally after hares. Should the stop watch become too much of a factor in Saluki assessment, we could be in danger of altering our beautiful breed for the worse.

For racing purposes, breeders of both Greyhounds and race horses have discovered that the straight hock and stifle are associated with the fastest dogs and horses *over a short distance.* To quote Mr. Smythe again "In both horse and dog there is not the slightest doubt that the ultra-short loin conveys a large degree of concussion to the vertebrae to such an extent that the stress experienced by the straighter stifled Greyhound puts them out of action after a comparatively small amount of racing" Our Salukis are meant to stay, to cover long distances, and to hunt fast and clever fit game over all sorts of country.

"Hocks low to the ground." Means very long hind legs — the hock in fact being the ankle of the dog. These long hind legs have two special functions: propulsion and reach. *Unlike* the horse this time, the Saluki and all the Greyhound family have very flexible spines. Using his nicely bent stifle, the Saluki pushes off powerfully with those long hind legs then bends his back so that his rear paws reach forward and strike the ground again well in advance of his front paws, making a series of tremendously long bounds and leaps. The pasterns (the bones below the ankle) should be sloping, to act as springs or shock absorbers as the feet hit the ground. This is often not obvious when the Saluki is standing still.

According to the Arabs the hock should be very pronounced and the lower the better.

As a result of the long hind legs, the main slope of the body, like that of an Arab horse, should be from tail to shoulder giving an impression of speed — the hindquarters being slightly higher than the shoulders. An arched back, but not a roached back, with spine showing is considered a sign of speed.

LOIN AND BACK *"Back fairly broad and muscles slightly arched over the loin".*

This is self explanatory. The fairly broad back means a good spring of rib for the chest within the first seven ribs plus room for all the dogs other essential organs (including puppy space for the bitch) which are contained under the last 6 pairs of ribs and to some extent under the seven lumbar or loin bones.

Above: **Champion Zebedee el Khizil.** Born in 1931, his breeding was mostly imported, and from the South.
(Photograph by Thomas Fall)

Below: **Hasana Sharqi,** a beautiful smooth Saluki, bred and owned by Mrs Barbara Abbott. She is a grand-daughter of the feathered Rihan (see page 81) mated to the smooth bitch Dhiba. The mating of smooth and feathered Salukis, a custom among some Arabs, is a matter of debate today.

According to the Arabs the loin should be very narrow. A man should be able to close his two hands round the loin of a Saluki, which should be strong and very well muscled. Many people exclaim in horror that young Salukis in particular often look so thin, despite being generously fed. Mrs Cecil Franklin of the one time well-known *Zahara* prefix used to say, "Provided your Saluki is well-muscled and firm over the loin, your Saluki is fit and there is no need to worry." This is confirmed too by Colonel H.R.P. Dickson who spent 16 years among Bedouin in the very instructive chapter on the 'Saluqi' in his book "The Arab in the Desert".

"The girth at waist must be fine – this for speed." Quite probably too, there is very ancient Biblical authority for this! In the book of Proverbs Chapter 30 we read, "There be three things that go well, yea four that are comely in going: the Lion which is strongest among beasts and turneth not away for any, a Greyhound, an He-goat, and a King against whom is no rising up."

Certain modern scholars argue that the word the 16th Century translated as Greyhound in fact means "girt in the loins". This is an Old Testament description of a man ready to run a long distance, i.e. "he girded up his loins". Comparatively modern travellers have told of Salukis likewise girt in the loins with broad leather straps! This would not restrict eating but it could well ensure maximum flexibility for galloping fast.

FEET *"Of moderate length, toes long and well arched not splayed out but at the same time not cat-footed, the whole being strong and supple and well feathered between the toes".*

It is a Saluki characteristic that the two middle toes on all four feet should be considerably longer than the two outer toes. The result is an oblong foot (not round like a cat's) and because the toes are arched the foot should look thick through in depth. The feathering is a unique feature occurring under as well as on top of the foot in order to protect it from the desert sand.

The Arabs want pronounced flatness of the rear paws showing easy quick turning at speed.

Constant exercise only on grass and soft ground is very bad for Saluki feet. In this country they need plenty of hard roadwork walking and a rough stone or clinker path along the fence of their home run can be very beneficial.

COAT *"Smooth and of a soft-silky texture, slight feather on the legs feathers at the back of the thighs and sometimes with slight woolly feathers on thigh and shoulders."*

Slight feathering, rather like a shirt ruffle, is sometimes found on the throat. A notable Saluki wearing this is Champion Bedouin Caliph.

COLOURS. *"White, cream, fawn, golden, red, grizzle and tan, tricolour (white, black and tan) and black and tan or variations of these colours"*

Any colour or combination of colours is permissible. Chocolate is a variation of red. The tribes originally bred Salukis to match the ground over which they hunted. Black and Tan is accounted for by black lava desert. As from time immemorial Salukis have been presented from one ruler to another as gift of honour, the colours must have been mixed and mixed again. According to Miss Amherst, "whole-coloured dogs with shading should be preferred." In a pale-coloured Saluki, a 'smoky' muzzle is said to be a sign of 'pure breeding'.

Part Two:
THE CONTROVERSIAL POINTS

EYES   *"Dark to hazel and bright large and oval but not prominent."*

The key words here are 'bright', 'large' and 'oval'. Most Salukis have eyes placed, like those of an Arab horse, halfway between the top of the head and the tip of the nose. Eyes contribute enormously to a Saluki's expression, which is important. In a general note at the end, the standard states "The expression should be dignified and gentle with deep faithful far-seeing eyes". The question of colour has been hotly debated, largely by people who were not members of the original committee in 1923. These original committee members are now no longer with us and we cannot ask them what connotation they put on 'hazel'. The hazel leaf is green — the hazel nut ranges from pale-green, through yellow and gold, to rich reddish brown according to ripeness. The Saluki a cream fawn imported from the Royal Kennels of Saudi Arabia had most beautiful golden amber coloured eyes and his sight was remarkable.

There is a prejudice — a pre-judging — about light eyes and not only in Salukis. But all Saluki lovers should be on their guard, as it is one of the points which chould change the breed without justification. Whether there is any correlation between long distance sight and eye colour is beyond the scope of this book but the golden eagle has a golden eye and so has the sparrow hawk — both far-seeing birds.

No Saluki should be penalised in the show-ring because of its eye colour *alone*. Light-coloured eyes in a dark dog may look incongruous, whereas the same colours in a pale coloured dog might not attract comment. In choosing between two hounds almost identical in conformation and Saluki character, any judge is entitled to exercise his preference, but it should be preference *other things being equal* and not advance-held prejudice.

For the following important paragraph on 'Eyes' by the well-known canine authority Robert Leighton writing in the 'Morning Post' of July 21st 1923, I am indebted to the Editors of the Saluki Club Magazine 'The Saluki'.

"The breed possessing the most searching and penetrating eyesight is the Arabian Saluki. In their native land these elegant swift-footed hounds are used for hunting the gazelle. Their power of distant vision is comparable with that of the condor (a South American vulture). They can detect their sand-coloured quarry miles away on the far rim of the desert, and it is interesting to note that their eyes are uncommonly pale with a golden topaz tint in the iris. They are brilliantly pellucid eyes, capable of staring into the fiercest sunlight without blinking. *The Bedouins greatly prefer a light eye in their gazelle hounds*" (my italics).

PAWS *"The paws should point forward at a small angle."*

This is another controversial point on which many judges will fault a good Saluki.

It is clearly stated in Miss Amherst's analysis of the breed, and also by Mrs Ester Bliss Knapp of Pine Paddocks, Valley City, Ohio, who also was presented with a Saluki bred in the Royal Kennels of Saudi Arabia. My authority for this is an article she wrote entitled "Judging Salukis" in the American Dog World of June 1955.

It makes sense to give extra purchase to an oval-footed hound travelling on loose sand.

TAIL *"Tail set on low and carried naturally in a curve, well feathered on the underside with long silky hair, not bushy".*

Miss Amherst's list of Arab requirements states "Tail feathering must be fine and regular. The tail when pulled down between the legs and round up the back should reach to the point between the hip bones".

Another good guide to the length of the tail is that the tip of the tail bone should normally reach the hock. The importance of this is that the tail is used as a rudder when the Saluki is running at speed.

To quote Mr Philip Richards again, "They were all very well feathered between the toes, enabling them to run fast, and safe and long on loose ground: also their tails carried abundant long hair which seemed to me to help them greatly on the turn and certainly greatly enhanced their beauty when moving at speed".

It should be noted that the standard says "Set on low" and "carried naturally in a curve". There is nothing about low carriage. The tail forms the final length of the spinal column and is a continuation of the sacrum — the last bit of the spine, so to speak inside the dog. It can be felt between the hip-bones which are themselves the upper end of the long sloping pelvis to which the sacrum is firmly attached and the slope of which it follows downwards. So the tail is low set. In the Arab horse on the other hand, the tail is high set because the pelvis and with it the sacrum are more horizontal than in the hound. The Saluki flexes his spine almost into a loop with his hind legs reaching right forward at the gallop. But the horse, having a much more rigid back bone, swings his legs at speed. The Arab horse carries his tail gaily, "at the least move, streaming in the wind like a cloak and this is considered a sign of breeding". A Saluki too at speed and at play carries his tail gaily and knowing as we do how closely the Arab equates his Saluki and his horse, there is plenty of evidence from imported hounds that this is the way the Arab likes a Saluki tail carried.

Further desert evidence comes in the early 1960's from people on leave from Saudi Arabia visiting the Branwen Kennels in Spain. Mrs Cynthia Madigan, an experienced judge, wrote at the time. "This couple have 3 Salukis: the feathered mother and a son and daughter both smooth, the Sire having been smooth. The male I admired particularly for his really outstanding conformation and soundness, wonderful angulation, fine head and great depth of chest. All three had quite tightly-ringed tails which, when I commented on them, I was told that is most particularly desired by the Arabs."

The writer's imported Saluki from Saudi Arabia's Royal Kennels also carried his tail curled. It went down to the more conventional position when offered a tit bit.

Standing and at a relaxed walk the Saluki usually does carry his tail in the low sweep which completes his elegant lines of curves from end to end. The tip of a Saluki tail frequently twists sideways in a final curl. In 1948, Major C.S. Jarvis writing in "Country Life" referring to the bas-relief of the tomb of *Ptah-Letep* at Sakkara, South of Cairo, dated about 2.500 B.C. notes that the Saluki there depicted had tails "tightly curled with a slight lateral tendency". He goes on "When the Saluki was introduced into this country in the late nineteen twenties, the earliest specimens which hailed from Iraq, then known as Mesopotamia, had long feathered and slightly curled tails so that this feature became established and was regarded as one of the essential points of the breed by those who judge dogs in show rings. I acquired my Salukis from the Trans-Jordan Bedouin about the same time and my dogs, which naturally I thought quite as good as those from Iraq that had obtained official recognition in this country, carried slightly feathered tails in a (tight) lateral curl. If ever I had appeared in the ring at Crufts with one of my Salukis with its very un-European tail, I expect I should have been ordered out again promptly! But I still maintain that my particular variety came of the old B.C. stock."

All these different positions are in fact 'natural curves' as the standard demands. Undoubtedly the comparatively low-carried tail looks to our eyes more elegant but it is equally certain that tail carriage is indicative of temperament. A nervous Saluki carries the tail tight under the body — relaxed, the tail hangs horizontally, but enjoying himself, which is much to be desired, the tail goes up, particularly when moving.

There seems no doubt that gay tails should not be penalised harshly if at all, nor, of course, should profuse feathering be allowed to outweigh any serious fault of confirmation.

Whiskers should not be cut. This is not part of the standard but to do so removes a typical breed characteristic. To quote again Colonel Dickson in The Arab of the Desert, "The dog with two hair warts under the chin is better than that with only one, and the one having three or four such hair warts is very good".

The exact function of whiskers is a mystery but our Salukis have them. As one small boy once said of Zahara Zuleika, who was good enough to win two Challenge Certificates before her untimely death, "Sally's got a face like a watering-can" and so she had, a watering-can in action!

In this connection it is interesting to note that Miss Amherst writing in or before 1907 in Cassell's new Book of the Dog refers to whiskers as "Smellers long — five warts defined".

HEIGHT   *"Should average 23 to 28 inches at the shoulders, bitches proportionately smaller".*

Five inches is an astonishing variation in size for any breed of dog, and no other aspect of Salukis confirmation has caused such controversy since the breed was registered at the Kennel Club. In 1933 feeling was running so high that it seriously affected Saluki entries at shows. Miss Desborough, a noted breeder and former Secretary of the Ladies Kennel Association, writing in Dog World states, "An exquisite type of hound, the lighter type, as it may have been called, has been consigned very much to the background by judges who have officiated for the last year or two. The owners of this lighter type no doubt prefer keeping their dogs away from the shows rather than to breed theirs to the heavier type in order to obtain a greater share of the spoils. One cannot possibly blame the owners — one might say the fortunate owners — of the lighter hound for retaining their slim elegance which, by the way is not a deficiency in build but an inherited fine quality handed down from generation to generation by many of the oldest tribes in the desert. One need not be in the least pessimistic about the popularity of the Saluki generally but from a show point of view, it will be necessary for the lighter type not to be deemed weedy but to be acknowledged as quite as correct as the heavier type, if entries are to be obtained in any numbers."

General Lance replied to this rather bitter letter, listing the imported dogs and remarking of the small ones that they produced big stock. As these had been mated to his own heavy stock, as we know from the pedigrees, it is not surprising!

There is I think a reasonable explanation and one I think too that holds a present day warning for the breed as a whole.

Writing in 1907, Miss Amherst puts the average height of a Saluki dog as 23 inches and that of a bitch as 21 inches, and weight Male 42lbs, Female 38lbs. She also states that because Salukis had been kept in Persia from the earliest times, Europeans tended to apply the term "Persian" greyhound to this variety and to infer that it originated in Persia. But, she points out, the Persian word for a Saluki is *Tazi* which in fact means *Arabian* — and the distinction *Shami* means *Syrian* which implies the feathered sort as distinct from the smooth which predominates in some districts of Persia. She states here too, and repeats it in another article some 20 years later, that "After two or three generations in Persia, Greyhounds become much bigger and heavier and have longer hair; sportsmen are therefore constantly *importing fresh stock from the south*". Why, if they were not better? She adds later "As with his famous horses and camels, the Bedouin attaches much importance to the pedigree of his Slughi or Saluki. Though different types are found in the same localities, natives are very careful not to mix the breeds. Some families of the Gazelle hound are specially renowned. A celebrated dog was looted as a puppy from South of Mecca. His descendants are now famous among the tribes of the north of the Persian Gulf."

We know that Miss Amherst had a scholarly, practical and almost life-long interests in the breed. There is little or no written evidence as to what Miss Mitchell thought after spending some 15 years in Egypt and Palestine. But she presented the Saluki Club with an Arab Trophy to be won at shows by the best Gazelle Type with such precise instructions that the lighter Saluki is clearly meant.

"For the best Gazelle type especially as to colour, expression of eye and elegance of moving. Size as to the standard of the Saluki Club".

We have the testimony of Colonel Dickson, who states, "The Bedouin Saluqi tends to be small: he is definitely a good deal smaller than the English Greyhound. Whether this is due to centuries of poor food I cannot say. Judging from the Arab horse born and bred in similar conditions, I should *say not* (my italics). I venture the opinion that just as the 14.2 and 14.3 Arab Horse of Arabia is the probable natural height of the original species, the far bigger thorough-breds found in Europe and America being un-naturally bred, so I should say that the small type of Arabian Greyhound should be considered as to conforming to the true standard of the breed and not the larger and much more powerful type found in Europe."

General Lance, who was a fairly near neighbour when I lived in Kent, was very kind to me when I was new to Salukis. He definitely wanted all Salukis to be big and strong and hefty. He was a regular soldier stationed in Syria. Regular soldiers do not as a rule spend more than 3-5 years in one district. Syria is well to the north of that vast area we term the Middle East and roughly speaking that North forms a large green crescent extending into Persia. It is mountainous: there is more rainfall, more vegetation, so game is larger, and hounds and horses need to be larger to match. Above all, General Lance was a Cavalryman, and Cavalrymen instinctively in horses, look for heavy bone and weight-carrying capacity. This spilt over on to Salukis where General Lance was concerned. It was also natural that judges in those early days should take his opinion as correct. He was a member of the Kennel Club and it was his enthusiasm for the breed which had won for it Kennel Club recognition. No wonder there was argument on the Saluki Club Committee!

It is only comparatively recently that people have come to realise not only how vast is the area of the Middle East, but also how different are the conditions there-in.

The late Mr McGregor Cheers writing in 'Dog World' some years ago made the point, "How many judging the Salukis as a Gazelle hound know the size of a gazelle or confuse it with that of a larger sort of deer? Gazelles vary in size with their district, but we have it on the authority by Brigadier Fitzroy McLean (his book Eastern Approaches) that in North Africa, where Salukis are also native, the Gazelle is the size of the Hare. In India, Gazelle are known as Ravine Deer. In Hindi they are called Chinkara and are chiefly found in all hot, dry and arid tracts. The Chinkara stands largely 28 inches in height".

Mr Philip Richards, who has been quoted before, stated, "I had at one time ten Salukis mostly brought from Mespotamia, and one big handsome cream dog which came West with refugees from Caucasus. They varied somewhat in type, bigger and more powerful the farther East and North their origin. But all were beautiful and one Poppay was the most graceful and lovely animal I have ever seen."

Colonel Dickson, in this connection, states, "The Arabian Saluqi proper must not be confused with his cousin the Persian Greyhound among Arabs; one of the best known Saluqi breeders and fanciers in Arabia was the late H.H. Shaikh Hamad bin 'Isa Al Khalifah, K.C.I.E., C.S.I., ruler of Bahrein.

Shaikh Hamad's Saluqis were however of a larger and more massive type than those ordinarily found among the tribes of the interior. Personally I am inclined to believe that Shaikh Hamad's Saluqis have Persian Greyhound blood in them or possibly were originally imported from the Persian Shore of the Gulf."

The Saluki presented by his Late Majesty King ibn Saud of Saudi Arabia to his Ambassador in London measured 25 inches at the shoulder.

In the writer's Kennel at the moment is a Saluki bitch who through her Sire is a granddaughter of Champion Bedouin Caliph and through her Dam a great granddaughter of a pair of Salukis bred by Sheikh Sabah Al Nasir of Kuwait. She is 23 inches at the shoulder.

We have ancient pictorial evidence of Salukis being carried on the back of an Arab horse. This would be impossible for a 28 inch tall Saluki on a 14.2 horse. Such a hound thus carried might even test the endurance of a camel and we have near contemporary evidence that this is how Salukis are carried in some districts.

The new sporting magazine in 1837 gave a vivid account of hunting the *Ghoo-phur*, or wild ass, in Persia on horse back with relays of 'Persian Greyhounds' up and down precipitous hills over stony paths and across ravines and mountain streams. On this sort of country a large strong hound would be essential.

So it would appear that the Saluki varies in size according to the work expected of him and the sort of country in which he lives and hunts.

No Saluki should be penalised in the show ring on account of size provided it is within the standard. Soundness, confirmation and elegance, should be the criteria. Like the Persian, we should endeavour to renew our stock from the South in pursuit of fine dense bone, intelligence, stamina, lightness and speed. The penalty for not so doing will mean the loss of the breed through sizing our hounds right out of the standard as we are at the present in danger of doing. To quote a show report by Mr. Brian Chambers after making Knightellington Vandal Best of Breed, "What I wanted I tried to be consistant in placing was the 'hard bitten' truly proportioned and wonderfully expressioned hound of the desert lands. I was looking for the most lovely hound type on earth, and yet these great show specimens were paraded so that at a little distance the poor bodies might have been mistaken for Labradors, especially when fawn coloured and some of the obese creatures were shown by exhibitors who should have known better!"

MOVEMENT. The standard of points says nothing about movement of a Saluki yet it is a very important characteristics of the breed. Saluki movement is quite different from that of a Greyhound. It is more springy when walking and at a trot it is more prancing. As one well-known judge put it, "Each step should look as though it were a push off for the next."

Basically in all breeds there are fixed rules on movement. When approaching the shoulders, elbows and forearms, the pasterns and feet must remain parallel with their fellows. There must be no punching out of the shoulders nor any slackness of the elbows. When going away from the observer, the same remarks may be applied to the stifles, hocks and pasterns. These must show straight parallel action, and there must be adequate stifle and hock flexion so that each leg is picked up smartly and the foot lifted and moved forward as the hock bends.

In the Saluki especially there must be a really good stride with the utmost economy of effort, no exaggerated high stepping but a good reach forward, and a strong propelling drive from the hindquarters. A far too common fault, as one specialist judge has put it, is knitting socks with the rear and scarves with the front!

Many people have tried to describe the typical Saluki movement. In notes from Lady Gardner, the second President of the Saluki Club, "Miss Amherst made a point that the Saluki should be lightly but strongly made and all its movement should be graceful" and again "The Nablous Salukis were not large hounds but they were full of grace. The Knightellingtons look to them as their forebears. We should, I think, have a care that our present day hounds do not grow too large and lose their graceful movement."

To quote Brian Chambers in another show report, "Are we losing sight of what constitutes typical breed movement? By this I mean that particular freedom of movement combined with extreme lightness and utter grace. Our breed should not be plodders."

The Flying Horse of Khansu. See opposite page on "Movement". (Photograph by Times Newspapers Ltd.)

Miss Patricia Kean of the *Ajman* prefix has described, "The really characteristic Saluki action .... light and with an element of dancing *not* wasting all the thrust by throwing the feet around, but giving the impression that the hound is almost air borne."

It may be added, in passing, that sometimes when walking relaxed the Saluki paces, advancing both right legs together and then both left legs. This, in the Saluki, is not a fault, it would appear to be a device for saving effort over a long distance. The camel moves like this and a variant of it is used by horses in the South African Veld.

Dramatic evident of the value of this type of movement for the Saluki was privided by the Chinese Art Exhibition of 1973 in London. The famous flying horse of Kansu is in fact 'pacing' (see illustration). No less an authority than the late Mr Henry Wynmalen was quoted in support of this mode of progression. At speed, all four feet are frequently off the ground together and the horse is, in fact, airborne.

THE SMOOTH VARIETY. *"In this variety the points should be the same with the exception of the coat which has no feathering".*
See photograph on page 43.

GENERAL APPEARANCE. *"The whole appearance of this breed should give an impression of grace and symmetry and of great speed and endurance coupled with strength and activity to enable it to kill gazelle or other quarry over deep sand or rock mountains. The expression should be dignified and gentle with deep, faithful far-seeing eyes".*

Colonel Dickson gives the following, from the Arab's point of view: "The Bedouin pays attention only to the following: –
- (a) The snout or muzzle must be long and narrow. This for breed.
- (b) The girth at chest must be deep – the deeper the better. This for staying power.
- (c) The girth at waist must be fine. This for speed.
- (d) The hocks must be well let down. This also for speed.
- (e) The width between the tops of the thigh bones measured on the back must be good, i.e. at least the width of a hand including thumb. This for speed."

4

Feeding your Saluki

4

FEEDING YOUR SALUKI

The most important ingredient for feeding your Saluki is common sense. *Your* common sense — his is almost automatic!

Basically a dog's needs are very similar to our own when it comes to food. We all need proteins for body building and repairing waste tissue, and fats and carbo-hydrates for producing energy and health. We also need Vitamins A.B.C.D.E. and probably many more besides, as well as trace elements of various minerals. There is in fact a lot in common between bringing up children and bringing up puppies! Even the measurement of food value can be calculated the same way, in calories (one calory being the amount of heat necessary to raise one gram of water by one degree centigrade).

Experts have calculated that a normal grown-up house dog needs 40 calories worth of food for every pound of his weight. So that a 30 pound adult Saluki would normally need 1,200 calories a day. When coursing, a Saluki would need more in the season, and growing puppies need nearly twice this calory rate per pound of weight, i.e. 80 calories instead of 40 per pound at certain stages of their development. A rough guide to the calory value of various foods has been worked out as follows: —

One Ounce of beef 50-100 calories; of mutton or lamb 70-80 calories; plain dog biscuit 100-125; wholemeal bread 70; whole egg 46; liver 40;

fresh milk 20; tinned dog foods about 50-55; lard 260; suet 262. So it is quite possible, with the help of a little arithmetic, to work out an adequate diet to keep your Saluki in good health, bearing in mind that a good *mixed* diet will probably supply the requisite amount of vitamins and mineral trace elements. There is very little vitamin A in lean meat but the oil of fish liver, egg yolk, milk, cream, butter and animal fat, liver and kidney all supply it. The valuable vitamin 'B' is found in yeast and wheat germ, i.e. wholemeal bread and good biscuit. Dogs manufacture their own vitamin 'C', the vitamin we get from fruit and vegetables. Vitamin 'D' comes in milk and is developed from carrots and cabbage and Cod Liver Oil. Vitamin 'E', the supposed fertility vitamin, comes from wholemeal flour usually included in Dog Biscuits.

So much for scientific theory about which every responsible person ought to know *something*. In practice, the supply of dog foods today is such big business that very high salaried research experts are employed by a number of firms to produce highly effective dog feeding at competitive prices, while still making at least a reasonable profit of course for the producers.

The emphasis at the time of writing is to produce convenience foods "all your dog needs" in one easy-served product. Dogs, however, like people, have individual tastes and they appreciate variety.

The aim is a good mixed diet, well-balanced as to essential ingredients. So it's as well not to mix two patent foods *in the same meal.* Similarly with additives — don't use more than one at a time. With 'complete' foods they should not be necessary and the all-important balance of the diet can be easily upset. Extra meat, 'innards', fish or both can be added to complete foods as a treat even if not technically necessary. They can be fed in larger quantities on their own or mixed with biscuit.

Generally speaking with dogs as with humans, "A spot of what you fancy does you good." The great thing is to watch your dog. If he is in hard muscular condition, energetic and cheerful, give him as much as he will eat with gusto, and when in doubt *consult your vet.*

A new puppy should come with a diet sheet from his breeder. The shock of changing homes is lessened if at least his food continues on the same lines. But don't forget to increase quantities as your puppy grows. Introduce changes in diet gradually. On the whole, Salukis eat well and because of their shape continue to look thin often till they are 3 to 3½ years old. A fully-grown fit Saluki should still show his hip bones and indicate 2 or 3 ribs. Salukis, more than other breeds, seem to concentrate a generous amount of food into building dense bone and strong muscles. As mentioned earlier, a man should be able to span a Saluki loin with his two hands, and a good firm muscle on the loin is indicative of Saluki health. As with other breeds you get the occasional 'poor doer'. If a *very* young puppy, new weaned or earlier, suddenly refuses to eat or suck, get him to a vet at once. Neat protein in liquid form can be prescribed and poured into him, with good results in a matter of hours. But at that age, a day's interruption in his feeding can put him way behind his litter mates, so that he must be fed by himself till he has caught up with them again in strength.

Suet (262 calories per ounce) either raw (your butcher will often give it to you free) or cooked in suet puddings is excellent for getting a Saluki to fill out. It's a great mistake to remove fat from meat fed to dogs, unless the vet orders a fat-free diet for some ailment. Remember too that a convalescent Saluki because of his desert origin will eat mutton or lamb in preference to chicken or rabbit. Breasts of lamb fed raw are always very popular and very nourishing. Bones should be given raw and preferably marrow bones. Never chicken or rabbit bones, of course, or any liable to splinter because sharp splinters can pierce the intestine and cause death. Fish is very good food value including fish bones which are more soluble than meat bones. A cod's head can be put through a mincer and makes a useful change. Herrings especially just baked in the oven and fed whole, bones and all, are very popular and nourishing.

We are apt to forget that dogs, even quite young puppies, have very strong digestive juices and that these juices should be given something to work on. Butcher's pieces are comparatively inexpensive and the various makes of frozen meats are very useful. Tinned meat and dried meat are valuable for emergencies as they keep indefinitely but where possible fresh food is preferable.

Given the chance, Salukis will graze almost like goats – couch grass and that sticky weed, bedstraw, being specially favoured.

Salukis are not big feeders or fussy feeders, but they require good nourishing food which need not be the most expensive. Miss Amherst's receipe from over 60 years is simple: "A good nourishing broth can be made of meat, onions, carrots and lentils or pearl barley and this poured over wholemeal bread is sustaining and appreciated".

So much for the present day food supplies. How were those very efficient Salukis fed in the desert?

It is sometimes argued that increased food supplies are directly responsible for the bigger Salukis we see around. This is very debatable. Lavish feeding of a 5ft man may make him fat; it will not make him into a 6ft man. Nor can it be suggested that the many owners of toy breed dogs in our midst keep them that way by starvation! The key is much more likely to be in selective breeding. The last 20 years in this country have seen an enormous increase in the number of Salukis entered in Shows, and a dramatic increase in the number of Shows which include Salukis in their schedules. There has not been anything like the same increase in judges with a specialist knowledge of breed points or the conditions in which the breed was originally reared.

There is a general tendency in all breeds for judges when in doubt to put up size! Consequently among exhibitors there is a tendency to mate big ones to big ones "because the judges like them" not realising that this way we could lose the breed.

Travellers tales tell us that the larger Salukis were to be found in the northern parts of the Middle East where hunting conditions demanded larger hounds. But just as the small Arab horse is valued in this country for the qualities he brings to thoroughbred stock and handy hunters alike, so the Saluki in Persia is known as *Tazi* and valued as "The Arabian" and we have plenty of evidence that in Arabia the Saluki is considerably smaller than their Persian cousins whose owners look to the south to improve their stocks.

As already stated, present day Veterinary opinion has commented on the contrast between the very dense fine strong bone of the small handy Arab horse and the larger and more porous quality of bone in the bigger breeds.

Tradition has it that the Saluki is the hound built like a horse. So the parallel is probably true.

What is the traditional economy of the Bedouin Arab? Again we refer to Colonel Dickson who has lived as one of them. "The average Bedouin has a hard and difficult existence. He seldom tastes meat — perhaps only when his Shaikh gives a dinner party. His own food for most of the year consists only of camel's milk and a handful of dates per day. Yet he is very very proud, valuing his Sharaf or honour almost above life itself, and he seems made of steel. In spite of his hard life the Bedouin is never in danger of actual starvation or of dying from want. His *ahl* (family) would never permit this nor would the system of affording three days hospitality to all and sundry — such a splendid feature of democratic Arabia — allow of a man reaching such straits. A Bedouin's dream and ambition in life is to possess (note the order and assuming that he starts with a rifle and a riding camel) about a dozen camels, next a wife, and afterwards a mare, half a hundred sheep and a Saluqi. Any male lambs that are born he kills for food — the females are kept for breeding. Young male camels are sold for food — only a selected few are retained to carry the household tents and baggage." That was written about 40 years ago.

Apart from dates and coffee, camel milk, *leben* (buttermilk), boiled rice, *semen* which is clarified butter made from sheep's milk, and sometimes a little bread formed the staple diet of even fairly prosperous Bedouin households. Only on very special occasions such as honouring an important guest would a lamb be killed, and the Saluki's contribution of hare or gazelle was a very welcome addition to the menu.

Nor was the Saluqi the only dog in the camp. "Every tent has its watchdogs which are fierce and very powerfully built. They guard the camels and sheep from wolves and strangers, and are trained to move round and round the tents all night in a large circle. The watchdog usually sleeps *outside* the women's apartments and is fed with little bits of rice, bread and dates left over from meals. *It is never allowed inside the tents, being unclean.* The Saluquis, on the other hand, are regarded as clean, and are allowed to enter the tents and sleep in the women's portion at will. Great care is taken that there shall be no interbreeding between the tent-watchdogs (the *Kelb*) and the Saluquis."

Quoting Miss Amherst again, "The Natives give great attention to the rearing of their Salukis. They bring them up for a year on sheep's milk which is said to make them strong and especially swift. When they are old enough, they are fed with the hawks. This almost certainly means that what meat they do get are the entrails, perhaps of the occasional sheep and more likely of desert rats, the Jerboa and other hawks' quarry. Certain it is that when not hunting the hawks will be fed only on meat not considered fit for Arab consumption – and that will not be very much!"

However inadequate we may consider a diet of milk, dates and rice, there can be no question that it keeps the Arab fit, as otherwise he would never survive such a very hard life, and if it did not keep the Saluki fit too, the Saluki would not be kept at all.

Clearly the key to the whole ancient Arab ecomony is milk, and the miracle of the centuries is the evolution of a race of camel, horse, sheep and goat capable of converting the very sparse dry vegetation of the desert lands into milk by way of meat. The result in man and hound may be small but it is sheer concentrated quality of steel like strength and stamina. Startling modern confirmation of this comes from the Sinai Desert as reported by Mr Thorn *(Tahawi Salukis)* in the Saluki notes for 'Our Dogs' from correspondence with a husband and wife Veterinary Surgeon team in 1970.

Following reports brought back by Israeli soldiers after the Six Day War, of light quick dogs living with the Bedouin Tribes, Dr. R. Trainer and her husband drove through Sinai in a jeep to seek out and photograph

Salukis.

The main tribe owning Salukis are the Tarabins. Since Sinai is a desert and half an island, Dr. Trainer thinks that very little influence has penetrated from the outside world for many thousands of years. The tribes are very poor, ride camels and have no horses. The goats are inbred and small and it appears that the Salukis are original without the influence of blood from Jordan or Syria although some fresh blood lines may have been introduced by the merchant caravans from Saudi Arabia which even today still travel these ancient trading routes.

These Bedouin appear to differ in many respects from these of Saudi Arabia and Kuwait, doubtless on account of geographical conditions. The women have to go off each morning with the sheep and the goats and the Salukis, returning in the evening.

There seems to be little now for the Saluki to hunt so his principal diet is dates fallen from the trees. "Although Dr Trainer (a Vet) considers this to be very poor nutrition *she admits that she never saw a dog with the slightest sign of under nourishment or ricketts.*" Moreover "Temperaments were excellent . . . . all were obedient and came to call on every occasion."

Perhaps more milk and dates would benefit our hounds here and now!

5

Training

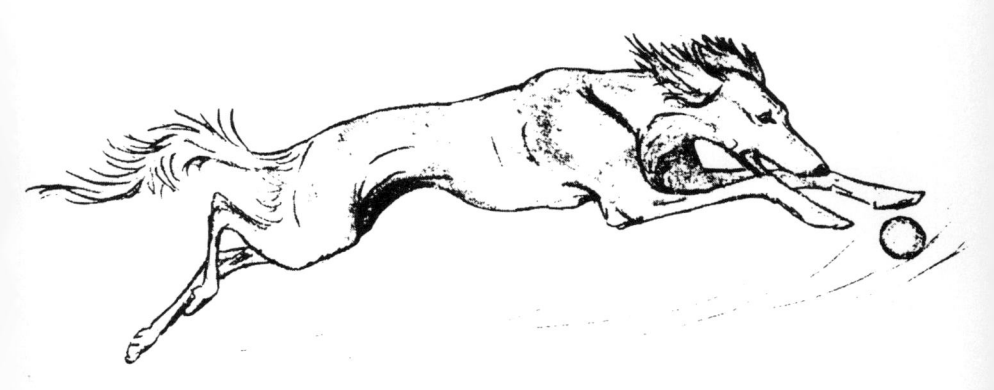

and Enjoying
your Saluki

5

TRAINING AND ENJOYING YOUR SALUKI

All companionship must be based on mutual understanding, affection and respect. Your Saluki has been bred as the companion of kings for something like 5,000 years. You will very soon discover that he tends to know it!

It has been well said that unlike some breeds which remain all their lives mentally dependant on 'Master' or 'Missis', the Saluki has an adult mind, which he is quite capable of making up for himself. If you happen to like what he is liking to do at the moment, that is just grand, but otherwise, well, his decision is final! The answer is quite simple: make sure that he likes what *you* want to do, and the key words are patience and praise. "According to the Bedouin the Saluqi is a particularly highly strung animal and should not be struck or whipped when being trained. Such treatment will definitely spoil and cow the hound, so the greatest patience must therefore be shown in training these hunting Saluqis of the Desert". Your Saluki is reserved, proud and sensitive but generous with his affection once he gives it.

He is also very intelligent but in unappreciative company this is not always apparent! He is slow to develop in body and mind but he carries his years lightly. He stays, in life as he does in the chase.

Of course, a young puppy properly treated adapts most easily to your way of life, but as one very experienced breeder put it, "I like older dogs: it's so very interesting watching their minds unfold."

Wherever possible Salukis should live in the house. When they must have outside quarters, they should be encouraged to run in and out of the house for the sake of their social education. There must be one place which belongs to your Saluki — his exclusively — box, bed or chair, preferably raised off the floor.

HOUSE TRAINING. This is of course the first essential. Puppies should be put out after a meal and always after a long sleep. Go with your pup and praise him for his performance. House cleanliness comes quicker if baby puppies are never shut in at night. They are naturally clean and as soon as big enough will always go outside if doors are not shut against them. Each Saluki has its own way of asking to go out. Some will stand by the door, some will put paws on your shoulders and get very confidential. *You* must be sensitive to pick up the message and act accordingly. A pool on a carpet is best dealt with by a newspaper trodden down to absorb liquid, followed by a quick mop with disinfectant solution, or better still a squirt from a soda water siphon to neutralise any staining acid. The Uric Acid in the pool is one of the oldest and best known fixatives for dyes. This is why dyers in the middle ages provided the first Public Conveniences. Salukis hate being unpopular. Usually disapproval in your voice, sometimes a light cuff, will convey the message 'mistake'. But it does happen occasionally with particularly highly-strung youngsters that the job is done immediately *on return* to the house. This is nerves, and punishment won't help. Understanding, immediate return to the garden, and time will effect a cure. A word here about outside and pavement training. Every dog's instinct is do his job off his own (i.e. your) premises and many people turn out the dog for this purpose and don't want to know more. In many areas especially where non-dog-owning gates are left open for car-users and on council housing estates that means a visit to someone else's lawn and inevitably makes for friction.

Lead your puppy to a special bit of *your* garden and preferably near the compost heap or the bonfire. He will soon get the message: the results will be easy to clean up and your compost heap will benefit.

When out on a walk, watch him in the early stages and nudge him into the gutter, or on to some rough ground when you see it to be necessary. Dogs should not foul pavements or childrens' playing grounds, and a little care is all that is necessary to prevent this.

COMING TO HAND. Freedom to use his legs is almost more important to any dog than freedom to eat his fill. This is specially so with a Saluki: he is a hound bred to chase anything that runs away, and your pleasure in watching a Saluki at speed is a very great pleasure indeed. For this reason it is vitally important that he should learn to come when called. It is also a very hard lesson for one so proud and independent to learn. Puppies should be handled and played with by as many people as possible from a very early age — preferably (say the experts) from 3 weeks onwards. When you get him at any age from 2-6 months make sure there are no holes in your garden fences and if the house is on a traffic-heavy road, a piece of wire netting attached under the gate or a concrete 'sill' is a wise precaution. Apart from taking him into the garden for obvious reasons make time to give him one or two or more short lesson periods every day. Let him get used to wearing a light collar to which you have attached a piece of blind cord as a trailing lead. Tie a piece of bright coloured rag to the free end of the trail lead so that you can see where it is. Play with your puppy — keep on calling him to you and *give him a tit bit every time he comes.* Ten or fifteen minutes is long enough for a lesson time to start with. If he doesn't come when called, put your foot on the end of the lead and haul him gently in, *making sure first that he can't slip the collar.* Reward and make a fuss of him and try again. If possible end the lesson on a success. Every time you call him use his names and the same word — i.e. "Come" or "Here". Some people say you should never use a puppy's name when scolding him. Then his name will always mean pleasure to him. *Never leave your puppy unaccompanied with a trailing lead.* If he ran away, he would get hung up on it and could hang himself.

The point of the trailing lead is partly to give you "remote control" but also to establish in his little mind that a collar and tie means "Fun". As he grows older you can take him for the same game in a large park or field (with the farmer's permission).

LEAD TRAINING. Once his innoculations are complete, you can extend the trailing lead lesson by picking it up and going for a short walk. He will almost certainly follow and equally certainly run ahead. Have ready a slip lead or light choke chain and a rolled up newspaper in your right hand. If he runs ahead persistently, a tug on the slip lead to bring him onto the 'heel' position, saying of course "Heel" will probably do the trick. If necessary repeat and reinforce by waving the newspaper in front of his nose. If he persists, tap him with it lightly. A rolled newspaper is a good dog weapon. They all hate it because they get it out of focus and it makes a noise. It doesn't hurt them.

THE ROUTINE WALK. All dogs love routine — they feel safe. Once your Saluki is fairly proficient at coming on the trail lead and walking on a loose lead, try to plan a regular walk which crosses a big open space, field, park or common which is free of livestock. Walk to the field, drop the trail lead, cross the field, let him run as much as he wants to, call him, pick up the lead and *continue the walk* home by another route if possible. It is important that coming to hand should *not* mean the end of the walk, but more fun and adventure.

When he is proficient on the trail lead, start again in the garden off the lead and progress as before.

CAR TRAINING. Whenever possible take your Saluki with you in the car: most of them love it. *Never* travel by car with dogs on a choke chain — preferably with no lead actually in the car, in case of accidents, but have the lead handy to put on before getting out.

A very young puppy may be sick the first two or three times, so be prepared with newspapers. Some Salukis however do take quite a long time to acclimatise to a car. The secret is to persevere. A very clever Vet has claimed that almost any breed can be cured of car sickness quite simply. "Fill the back of the car with sacks and newspaper and drive the dog around continuously for three days"! Drastic perhaps, but effective, because car-sickness is a form of nerves and three days is long enough to convince a dog that nothing more alarming happens and car-travel is not really so bad. Show Salukis may be sick on the way *to* a show but never coming home!

Of course, being sick is not such a disaster to a dog as it is to a human. It is merely making a tummy more comfortable. Another method is to use a mild tranquiliser on 2 or 3 occasions, then half the dose and gradually leave it off. Give your Saluki some comfort in the car and be sure he is protected from draughts. The bare floor of an Estate Car is cold and hard on a long journey and the inevitable jolting, however mild, is very tiring. Never let his head hang out of the window. Apart from being bad for his eyes, the cold air is damaging to his lungs.

The car, if you have one, should be your Saluki's second home. It gets him out into the world and educates him in traffic and people. It also gives you and him more scope for walks. *Your Saluki will always come back to the car* if he left you at the car, just as he will always come home if he is lost on a walk from home. In this connection the writer was told an amusing story about an owner walking his Salukis from his car on Dartmoor. Suddenly the local hunt appeared on the horizon. Off went the Salukis, through the horses, through the hounds, despatched the fox and returned to the car, to be met thankfully by a very worried owner who drove off quickly before awkward questions could be asked!

IF YOU LOSE YOUR SALUKI. He will always come home *if he can*, but he may meet or get into trouble on the way. His homing instinct, born of the desert, is very strong indeed. A new owner of any Saluki over 4-5 months must take very special care to convince the dog that the new home is the real home. Outside a well fenced garden, a lead is essential for at least 2 weeks, otherwise he will try to get back to the kennel where he was born. If he fails to find his way home, he will eventually come back to where you lost him *because you are his only point of contact with his original owner.* Two young men bought a grown Saluki bitch and took her to a new home 60 miles away. Despite warnings from the breeder to keep her on the lead for a fortnight, they let her off in the garden on the second day "because she had been so good in the house." Immediately she was off, found a hole in the garden fence and disappeared into a surrounding forest. Acting on instruction from a panic phone call to the breeder, they waited, having of course informed all the local people they could think of. Two days later she was seen briefly outside the garden. In the quiet of the third night she slipped into the kitchen. And two sleepless but relieved young men pulled a string to shut the door behind her! She never attempted to run away again and could be taken for walks off the lead happily and securely.

Another story concerns a Saluki sold to Sweden. He became devoted to his new master but only tolerated the rest of the household. Came a day when Master fell ill and was taken to hospital for a long period. Despite every care, the Saluki got out and tried to find him. Of course he failed but though he haunted the neighbourhood for weeks and people put out food for him, he would not be caught. Eventually he was captured at the airport, several miles distant, under the wing of a plane about to take off for England!

LEAVING YOUR SALUKI AT HOME. There are times when any dog must be left at home alone.

So train your puppy by leaving him somewhere secure for short periods, say half an hour to start with and gradually extend the time. But when you leave him, give him something legitimate to chew or tear up. Until convinced that you are really coming back, your Saluki will first try to get out and can be very clever at opening doors and windows. Once he finds himself defeated in this, he won't try again. But having failed, he may from sheer panic and frustration chew and tear furniture or anything handy. Those two famous names in the pedigrees, Champion Mihjan Khodama and his litter sister Champion Johara Cheetah, were reared from birth in a small cottage. On occasions when they had to be left in the one sitting room, Mrs Vivien Riley always provided 2 or 3 cartons, a newspaper and a piece of knotted rope. On her return the room looked a shambles but was easily cleared up and the furniture was safe!

YOUR HALF-GROWN SALUKI. Salukis can be trained to a quite extraordinary degree, some cheerfully and very quickly, but with others it takes time and it takes patience. As a breed, they are also very late developers and do not come to their best until 4 or 5 years old. They are naturally reserved and stand-offish with strangers, and once out of puppy-hood many are too proud to be bribed. Windswift Nathan always fetched the newspaper from the front door and carried it unharmed to master still in bed.

Windswift Tabitha would catch recalcitrant geese by holding them firmly but gently with paws on their backs till master came to collect them. She would also, for her own convenience, turn on the radiant heat (from a cord in the middle of the room) and then go over to the bed and lie under it!

Goldendawn Sakbar had free range in the house and grounds of the Hotel de Paris at Bray. She was trained never to go in to the public rooms. Though the doors especially in summer were nearly always open, she would just stand and look in and wait for her owners to come out.

Windswift Agag and Hanifa, both dogs, lived in a tiny Georgian terraced house in Tunbridge Wells. With no garden, it opened straight onto a steep cobbled lane leading up from a busy high street and also from the main London to Coast Road, across which was the common where they had free run every morning. On command they would stay loose in the open doorway of the house while their owner went shopping, serenely confident that her house would be cool on a blazing summer day and no-one, repeat no-one, would get in till she got back.

Taufaan Sharqi regularly took complete charge of his owner's baby grand-daughter and evolved a special bark, used for nothing else, which said "Human aid needed — I can't cope!"

Sabbah, straight from the Desert, would stop younger Salukis chasing livestock by 'riding them off' as though playing Polo.

Nevertheless, a great many Salukis do go through an awkward patch between puppy hood and full maturity (somewhere around 9 months to 2 years old). They grow out of it, but while it lasts it can be maddening. Bold friendly puppies will suddenly become nervous and shy. A usually biddable youngster becomes impossible to catch. At this age too they can move fast and far which is why it is so important to train them to come to hand continously from a very early age. Increased shyness at this age has been described as a psychological requirement of nature to guard them against more trouble than they can cope with, because though looking grown-up they are still without the basic strength which full maturity brings.

At this stage the more you take them round with you on a lead in crowded places the better. As so many shops now refuse to admit dogs, it may mean a special expedition for your Saluki's walk but it will be worth it. Traffic, Woolworths, or markets on crowded afternoons, just walking up and down a busy street several times a week, brings great improvement even if slowly. Training classes are excellent because they meet other dogs doing the same thing. Salukis, remember, are apt to be as stand-offish with other breeds as they are with humans.

If your local training class only trains for orthodox 'obedience' and not ringcraft, ask the instructors to include teaching the command 'Stand', otherwise you may find yourself in the Show ring with a Saluki who 'Sits' because *you* are standing still, awaiting the verdict of the Judge!

A lovable impulse for mischief, combined with acute sensitivity to your mood accounts for most of the serious disobedience trouble.

To overcome it, you need considerable mental self-control and foresight. Allow plenty of time to call your Saluki to hand, in the garden or on a walk, if you have an urgent appointment elsewhere.

The emotions of the rider travel down the bridle to the mind of the horse. But your Saluki needs no bridle. First he senses your tension and plays it up for fun, then he knows you are getting angry and apprehension takes over, eventually he really wants to come to you, but his pride won't let him. Then comes a really critical battle of wills and *you must win.* The first will be the worst and soon there will be no more.

Like any other naughty child, your Saluki hates being 'ignored'. If on a walk he is racing away from you and won't come to your call, turn and walk in the opposite direction *and don't let him see you looking back.* If he has got a long way away from you, try to determine whether he is running towards left or right. Usually, like a hare, he runs in a big circle and in open country you can often take a short cut and meet him! You may not be able to catch him immediately, but you will almost certainly find him following fairly close. If it's safe traffic-wise to go home, he will follow. If not, sit down on a stone or tree-trunk, take no notice of him and wait. He will come to you eventually. Then is the time to make a tremendous fuss over him when you have got him on the lead. In the garden when he won't come in, go in yourself, be busy with something else, leaving the door ajar. When he does come in, take no notice till you can safely get between him and the door to shut it, and then make a fuss. *Never never* let your exasperation lead you into scolding him, or worse, punishment when he has eventually come to you! If you are a good enough shot to hit him with a thrown lead or lump of earth when he is *actually running away* despite your call, that is very salutary and he will understand. But to hit him when he has at long last obeyed you is fatal, he won't trust you again.

TRAINING TO LIVESTOCK. Your Saluki is a hound. His natural instinct is to chase whatever runs away. To start with, it is play and he looks magnificent. Often from sheer exuberance he runs through a herd of cattle or flock of sheep and is not chasing. But the farmers won't see it this way. A cow can slip her calf or break a leg. Sheep can lose lambs or die of heart failure and the financial loss is very serious, and can't be made good for a year at least. If he chases a horse, it can kick and kill him out in a field though most likely it is trained to hounds and won't budge. But a sudden aggressive encounter on a road could make a horse shy and cause a bad accident involving loss of human life. To train your Saluki seek the co-operation of a friendly farmer. *With his permission* lead the dog regularly in among cattle and sheep on a choke chain and a firm command "Leave" every time he looks at an animal will make your point, but don't expect results at once. Give cows with calves a very wide berth indeed. In defence of her calf, the usually docile cow will attack. The hound will get away and she may well turn on you and can be very very dangerous.

To round off your sheep-training, plan an encounter in a small pen between your Saluki (on a choke chain) and a ewe with lambs. She will attack the Saluki, butt him repeatedly into a corner but the butting will only frighten him and not damage him.

Free-range chickens are another hazard. If you live in the country, train him in your own hen run under supervision as a tiny puppy if possible. One final warning. However well you think your Saluki is trained, be extra careful in strange country. The sheep and cattle and hens he meets at home are probably regarded as your property and to be left alone. But strangers' property may be another matter: either they are not yours or being a different breed in different country, they smell different!

When all is said and done, cheerful obedience at coming to hand can be worth literally many hundred of pounds. Insuring your Saluki against Third Party Risks is a very well worth-while precaution. Such an insurance is in fact at the time of writing written in to membership of the Saluki or

Training and Enjoying Your Saluki

Gazelle Hound Club.

It is sometimes remarked that Salukis have much more confidence in women than men. This is only true where they meet no men in the household as young puppies. Where a man takes sole charge of his Saluki puppy, he wins its affection and loyalty from the start of his ownership. But usually the Saluki has to be left at home for the wife to look after and, being small and simple, it adopts one loyalty at a time.

It may of course also be something of an age-old instinct. In the Desert, the Saluki frequents the women's side of the tent where it is fed. The women tend the whelping bitch, digging a deep hole in the sand as a nursery to keep her cool by day and warm at night. The children educate the baby puppies teaching them first to retrieve bones and desert rats thrown for them. At about six months old they are taken out to hunt rats and Jerboa. They are subsequently taught to course hares and finally gazelle. At two years old they should be fully qualified for sport.

A very valuable book on Field training for dogs generally is "Tell Him" by Lt. Colonel Badcock. He is particularly interesting on the use of the long lead, and maintains that most dogs can be efficiently trained by obedience to just five words: "Come – Sit – Stop it – Leave – and Hi-On".

Certain it is that by working together, every day, indoors and out and in all weathers on some such training programme as this, you and your Saluki grow to an absorbing understanding of each other which spells enjoyment and companionship for both of you of a very high order. It pays off in the show ring too. The record-breaking Saluki dog Miss D. Steeds' Bedouin Caliph who has won no less than 24 Challenge Certificates comes into the ring with such obvious confident enjoyment in his owner's companionship that his whole personality glows from every whisker. He *has* to win.

Continuously too, you will be meeting with living signs of an ancient lineage. Heads go up to watch a bird or an aircraft overhead: once they were trained to follow a hawk when they lost sight of the gazelle. The star on some foreheads has been regarded by Arabs for centuries as a protection against 'The Evil Eye'. A cluster of white hairs on shoulder or withers is a speed mark similar to the thumb of the prophet mark in an Arab horse.

And most convenient of all for us today, such great and rather drastic care has been taken (for centuries) to avoid any crossmating between the 'unclean' Kelb or watchdog for the herds and the Saluki – the gift of Allah for hunting – that even other dogs today find the Saluki something different. If your Saluki is a bitch, you will find that dogs of other breeds take hardly any notice and you don't get 'followers' when she is in season. This of course does not necessarily apply when the 'dog of another breed' actually lives in the house with her.

Saluki bitches make very good mothers and usually whelp easily. The late Lady Gardner told the writer how her first Saluki "Dream of Delight" bred by Miss Mitchell, though never bred from herself, brought up three Irish Wolf hound puppies and "simply worshipped them." She added, "This is in keeping with a story Miss Amherst used to tell of a Saluki bitch leaving a gazelle hunt to suckle a new born fawn that she heard crying for its mother."

6

Coursing your Saluki

6

COURSING YOUR SALUKI

Whatever your views on coursing, there is no doubt that it is the very ancient sport for which your beautiful hound has been perfected.

To preserve the breed, this historic instinct should not be allowed to decay.

For sheer enjoyment, a fine day out on the downland moor or field watching a score of owners strung out across a hillside each with one or two Salukis in leash, all raring to go after the brace just slipped after a hare is a sight not easily forgotten. The object today is not the killing of the hare (many in fact get clean away) so much as the testing of the hounds at the job for which the Almightly created them.

Moreover, walking with your now well-trained Saluki in the country, even on a country road, you may easily 'put up a hare' and, like it or not, you have some private coursing on your own!

Hares sit tight on their 'forme' in the open field and because there is no scent until they move, you can easily stumble over one before it moves and then it moves fast. So will your Saluki! Two things are important to remember. First, on country walks always carry a stout stick. Your Saluki will catch a rabbit, hare or even a pheasant and may not kill it immediately. This you must do at once for humane reasons. Hold the rabbit by the hind legs and give a sharp blow behind the ears.

Second, if your Saluki does kill any game when out walking, the hare (or whatever) technically belongs to the owner of the land you were on at the time and should be offered to him. Otherwise it is poaching, and though there is a spice in poaching, you ought at least to know the rules. Near at home anyway, it's advisable to establish friendly relations with the farmers over whose land you like to walk. They will probably take an interest in your Saluki's hunting ability and let him get some practice.

If you decide to take up coursing seriously, you should acquire a set of double slips. This is a special pair of collars with a hollow lead containing a second lead. One hound goes into each collar until you put up a hare, then the inside lead is given a sharp pull and both collars fall open simultaneously when both hounds have sighted the hare, who has been given a really good start. Double slips are regulation for normal coursing and it's important that your Saluki should get used to being coupled up with a strange hound and know the work expected of him.

At the time of writing, the Saluki or Gazelle Hound Club has a very flourishing coursing section and details can be had from the Secretary whose address can be found at the end of this book.

There are many references in Arab literature to the "fine trained lop-eared hounds with slender sides who lightly out-run the sharp-horned white antelope."

Here are three accounts of coursing Salukis from three different areas of the Middle East which indicates how varying conditions demand different types of hound.

From Colonel H.R.P. Dickson in Kuwait:
"The Saluqi is kept primarily for hunting and is taught to run down hare and gazelle. The best of these hounds are capable of going out alone short distances from camp killing and bringing back to their master any hare they can put up. I have in mind a beautiful grey Saluqi bitch belonging to Shaikh Salim al Hamud al Subah of Kuwait, which used frequently to go hare-hunting on her own when her master was in camp, and two days out of six she would bring back game. She was an exception however."

From the late Mr M.V.S. Henderson in Iraq:
"I was invited to many Gazelle hunts. The food of the Saluki in the desert is in the main, dates and rice with the odd lump of mutton, beef, gazelle or chicken depending on the state of the larder. The area which we hunted was exceedingly flat with here and there shallow undulations. The Saluki on being released manoeuvres along the undulations, practically crawling along the ground, until he has worked himself closer and closer to

Kumasi Rihan, imported from Iraq (see page 13). This dog had killed 42 gazelle before coming to England.

the herd. He then crouches down and watches the herd, appearing to me to be picking out his quarry. He then lunges forward and the chase begins, sometimes covering two or more miles, the hound never giving up until he has made his capture by which he stays until his master or keeper arrives. When the gazelle is killed and cleaned, the hound gets the heart as his reward. It was very noticeable that the Saluki will pass many gazelle during the hunt but does not swerve from his purpose to catch the one of his choice."

Lastly from an article on the Persian Greyhound appearing in the 'New Sporting Magazine' for September, 1837:

"This species of greyhound is much esteemed in Persia where the nobles who are excessively fond of the chase keep a great number of them at considerable expense, the best and most favoured dogs frequently having collars and housings covered with precious stones and embroidery. These greyhounds are employed in coursing hares in the plains and in chasing the antelope.

The chase however in which the Persians chiefly delight and for which these greyhounds are most highly valued is that of the Ghoo-Phur or wild ass. This animal which generally inhabits the mountainous districts is extremely shy of great endurance and is considered by the Persians one of the swiftest of all quadrupeds. Its pursuit is extremely hazardous.

When the Persians go out to hunt the wild ass, relays of greyhounds are placed at various distances in the surrounding country in such directions as are most likely to be traversed by the object of pursuit, so that when one relay is tired there is another fresh to continue the chase. Such however is the speed of the Ghoo-Phur that it is seldom fairly run down by the greyhounds, its death generally being achieved by the rifle of some lucky horseman. The Persians evince great skill and courage in the arduous sport, riding, rifle in hand, up and down precipitous hills, over stony paths and across ravines and mountain streams which might well daunt our boldest, turf-skimming Meltonians."

7

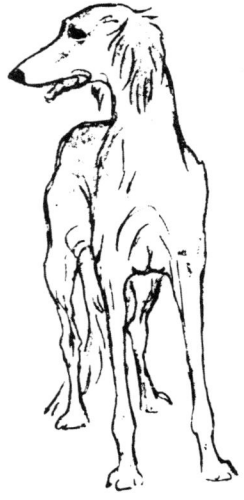

Imported Salukis

7

IMPORTED SALUKIS

The following account of imported Salukis divides naturally into two groups: pre-war (up to 1939) and post-war (1946 onwards).

The Honourable Florence Amherst was given a brace of Saluki puppies from the Sheikh of the Tahawi Tribe (a branch of the great *Anizeh*) in the Saliha Desert, Egypt, by Colonel Jennings Bramley in 1897. From contemporary eye-witnesses and later admirers of the Amherstia prefix, we can deduce that these were the fine-boned lighter variety. From the photograph showing two Amherstias with Miss Amherst, it would appear that these were about 25 inches at the shoulder.

Brigadier General F.W. Lance imported Sarona Kelb from Syria and a bitch Sarona Rishan who was bred by the Vali of Pushti Koo in Central Iraq. We do not know the height of these Salukis but they were evidently fairly tall, definitely 'sizeable' and judging from personal experience of General Lance's taste in Salukis, they were comparatively heavy in build and the heaviness tended to accentuate as they grew older. Both Syria and Iraq border on Turkey and the latter on Northern Persia. In other words they lie in the far north of the territory where Salukis are found. General Lance also imported Sarona Kataf bred by Daud Bey el Doghastani of the Shammar tribe.

Major Bentinck imported the Saluki Dog Rishan and a bitch Feena from Mosul in Northern Iraq. Hama of Homs came from Northern Syria.

Above: Champion Sarona Kelb, at an advanced age. Imported by Brigadier Lance from Syria.
(Photograph by Thomas Fall)

Below: Champion Knightellington Caspah, aged 11 years. Most of his forebears were the lighter type from the South.

Mrs Crouch, of the Orchard Prefix, imported Hoshan from Bahrein, and a Major Philby imported a bitch Hosha and three others, one of which may have been Abu Souffi also from Bahrein. Although Bahrein is an island well to the south of the Middle East area — i.e. Persian Gulf, we know from Colonel Dickson that the ruler in the 1920's, Sheikh Sir Hamad bin Isa al Khalifah K.C.I.E.C.S.I., owned a fine kennel of Salukis which were larger and more massive in type than the Salukis on the Mainland. Colonel Dickson suggested that these Salukis "had Persian Greyhound blood in them or were imported from the Persian side of the Gulf." He added that they did little or no hunting and were fat rather than muscular.

The type of heavy hound thus described certainly fits the Orchard prefix as shown in the pictures that have come down to us.

Of the lighter type, Mrs Vereker Cowley imported Malik el Zobair who was bred by the Montific Sheikh who rules in Southern Iraq near the northern end of the Persian Gulf and also Zobeida el Zobair who was bred by Sheikh el Zobair which lies still further south near Basra.

Miss Joan Mitchell imported Ebni and Binte el Nablous whose sire was Mr Hensman's Jack of Jerusalem and whose dam was Sheila of Amman. These were definitely the smaller lighter type. Miss Amherst is also said to have imported Salukis from this source. Miss Mitchell presented the Saluki Club with a trophy, an Arab water jug and basin still competed for annually "For the Best Gazelle Type." The stated condition being, "For best of lighter type. The winner to resemble the deer, gazelle or fawn for colour, eye and elegance in movement." At some time Miss Lucy Bethell of Newton Kyme Tadcaster imported a bitch from Wadi Sirhan which lies south of Jordan, through the Shammar country bordering on Saudi Arabia. Presumably therefore this bitch was similar in type to those from Jerusalem and Amman.

Miss Aline Doxford founded her kennel of Salukis in Sunderland with a beautiful Grey Saluki bitch, Tazi, which was given to her by an army officer who had owned her while campaigning in the Egyptian desert — geographically in the same latitude as Saudi Arabia. This bitch, evidently similar in colour and habit to that referred to by Colonel Dickson as belonging to the Sheikh of Kuwait, was out hunting on her own when the detachment was ordered to move camp. *She followed her master over 100 miles alone across the desert* to an eventual joyful re-union!

Close study of the Kennel Club files between the wars would reveal more imported Salukis. But those mentioned are sufficient to show the basis of the fierce argument that developed about Saluki type.

As already mentioned, the pedigrees show that there was inevitably cross-mating between the Amherst Lance-Crouch Mitchell-Cowley strains. It was also inevitable that, lacking our present much wider knowledge of the Middle East, Judges would tend to follow a fellow member's ideas on the breed he had introduced to the Kennel Club and habitually awarded top honours to the larger type.

In the young dog, the difference in type is not so apparent. The late Miss Gullan Lindroth whose famous El Saluk Kennel in Germany was founded on her Sarona purchases from General Lance, used to say that the original Saronas did not, to her, appear heavy. The two photographs, one of Champion Sarona Kelb at an advanced age, and one of the equally used Champion Knightellington Caspah (who though tall is finely built) aged 11 years, show the difference in type. The photo of Champion Naomi el Hor taken some time after she had been made up, shows her close relationship to Sarona Kelb who was behind her breeding some 18-20 times! It is probable that almost every Saluki bred in England today has Kelb at the back of its pedigree, to a greater or lesser extent. Nablous Farhan who sired Lady Gardner's very elegant finely built red Knightellington Salah-ed-Din was the grandson of 4 imported Salukis, Malik el Zobair, Zobeida el Zobair, Champion Sarona Kelb, and Binte el Nablous, i.e. Kelb once only. The dam of Salah-ed-Din had no Kelb in her pedigree at all, but she was both the daughter and grand-daughter of Binte el Nablous. Mazuri Bedouin, a forebear of Naomi el Hor, was a much used sire in his day and had Kelb behind him some 14 or 15 times.

Both Bedouin and Naomi are post-war Salukis.

Success leads to success, and like produces like. During the war most dog breeding stopped, but Mrs Gwen Angel, whose service to the breed has been considerable through informed correspondence and her notes in 'Dog World' for many years, managed to carry on her Mazuri prefix, and Mazuri Bedouin who was very like Sarona Kelb was much in demand as a Sire in the late 1940's. Naomi el Hor was one of many champions bred by Mrs Coston whose kennel was founded on Mazuri Bedouin stock. Miss Eaton's Golden Dawn Ra'ad, a son of Zahara Felicidad and Bedouin, produced Champion Pharaoh el Hor, a Saluki of very impressive size indeed. A visit to the El Hor Kennels showed that the majority of the prefix were definitely big and heavy in type.

One of the earliest post-war Saluki imports was bred by Mr T. Creighton in Berlin from German stock. Burydown Uki originally belonged to Miss Elizabeth Wyndham of Petworth House, who gave him to Mrs Hope Waters.

He has made a very great contribution to the breed, largely on account of his excellent temperament. But he brought in no new Arab

Above: Nablous Farhan. Grandson of four desert-imported Salukis, and great-great-grandsire to Ch. Knightellington Caspah (see p. 86). (Photograph by Thomas Fall)

Below: Champion Naomi el Hor. She has Ch. Sarona Kelb 18-20 times in her breeding. (Photograph by Thomas Fall)

blood. He was, with one significant exception, a re-introduction of British blood lines, most of them Sarona bred through Miss Lindroth's el Saluk Kennel. The exception, ten or twelve generations back, was Cyrus and Slougha Peri, a pair imported from Persia, where as already mentioned Salukis tend to be the larger variety.

Uki was mated in the first place to Burydown Saladina whose dam Tala Hinna Anida also had a lot of Sarona blood behind her, but whose Sire Knightellington Eaglet came from Lady Gardner's Knightellington Daragi and Knightellington Barake, a pair of beautifully-made but much smaller finer type of Salukis.

Uki repeated Kelb's achievement in that his stock was very successful in the show ring, with the result that he and his stock have been used extensively at stud and it is now quite difficult to find a Saluki which has not got Uki several times in his or her pedigree!

Probably because of this, a great many judges have so to speak 'got their eye in' to a much larger and heavier type of Saluki and the smaller finer specimens which are well within the standard and meet with Arab requirements for the breed have been designated too small.

However during the 1950's and 1960's there have been several very interesting Arab imports, most of which come from the south, and are smaller and probably nearer the original Saluki stock.

Mention has already been made of Sabbah the Windswift bred in Saudi Arabia by a nephew of his Majesty the late Abdul Aziz ibn Saud who presented him as a traditional mark of honour to the Saudi Arabian Ambassador in London, His Excellency Sheikh Hafiz Wahaba. Sabbah was 25 inches at the shoulder.

Ghazala Miseryah bred by Sheikh Abdullah al Khalifa of Bahrein was imported by an Army Officer and is now owned by Mrs Angel. He is 25½" at the shoulder. Reference has been made also to the late Mr Henderson's feathered Kumasi Rihan bred by Sheikh Shakar of Iraq. Rihan had already pulled down 42 gazelle before being presented. Imported with him was the smooth bitch Kumasi Dhiba bred by Sheikh Chassib Miftin also from Iraq. She was 23" tall, the lowest limit of the standard for a dog but well within it for a bitch.

Also in the 1950's, Mr and Mrs. Heard imported a pair from Kuwait: Taufaan 25 inches tall and Najma Min Sharq 24", both being bred by Sheikh Sabah al Nasir of Kuwait. This pair produced a litter of puppies while still in Kuwait, and one Sabah al Kuwait was imported into England independently by his new owners. He was shown quite successfully and sired some good stock. Taufaan Sharqi, from a later litter, is also sire and grandsire of many prize-winning hounds.

Mrs Lees imported a pair with their progeny from the Lebanon which, mated to English stock, have produced some very good showworthy hounds.

Caesar Rualla 24 inches tall, was bred by the Emir Fauz Sh'allan and the bitch Amira Razzaka, 22 inches tall, was bred by Sheik Abdul Razzak al Razzouk.

The bitch Falha Rualla was also imported by Mrs Lees, and her litter sister Bjonnarie Ferial was brought in by Mr Jonathan Horswell. Nanajan Shamoon was a smooth bitch imported by Professor and Mrs Seton Lloyd but died after producing only one litter. Caroline of Gaza was another import which appears in the pedigrees and whose name indicates her origin well to the south, bordering on the Negev Desert.

Lastly Taverton Rhumli Saggers imported from Saudi Arabia is another fine boned dog of substance yet only 24 high. He was bred by a Bedouin Tribe and, mated to a daughter of another Arab import Bjonnarie Ferial, has already produced stock which is being placed in the show ring.

"To ensure the continued purity of the breed" the contribution made by these Salukis imported from lands where conditions still approximate to those of the Patriarchs, is very important indeed. Without them we are in danger of changing, albeit imperceptibly, the Saluki of the Desert into an artificial creation — a Saluki of the show ring. Owners of Salukis imported *from their land of origin* should be encouraged to compete for Miss Amherst's Trophy — the striking replica of Benevenuto Cellini's bas relief — presented for the best Imported Saluki, at the Saluki Club's Open Show (open to all) in order that as many Saluki owners as possible should see the imported types and learn from them. Quite recently Miss Vivan Bonander who first introduced Salukis into Sweden and who, like her great friend (also Swedish though living in Germany) the late Miss Gullan Lindroth (el Saluk), had bought her Salukis from General Lance was shown a pair bred from pure Kuwait stock. She was amazed. Over many years, her eye had become accustomed to the developing variation as the breed had developed on the continent where Arab Salukis, the original types themselves, cannot be registered!

She was also extremely interested and her long experience appreciated the basic Arab qualities of these hounds and their compliance with the standard of points, although they looked different from the Salukis she knew in Sweden.

Finally, as a modern indication of what expert Arabs look for, the photo on page 25 is of interest. In the early 1960's, the ruler of one of the larger Persian Gulf States sent one of his London agents, plus a party of Arabs, one of whom obviously had special Saluki knowledge, to buy a pair for his own kennels. The party toured most of the Saluki breeders at least in the South of England and made one or two purchases for other Sheikhs in the area. But for the ruler, these two were selected: descendants of Sabbah the Windswift from Saudi Arabia mated to a bitch carrying the best British blood lines of her day. The taller of the two, the bitch, was not more than 25 inches.

To sum up, we must all realise – Breeders, Judges, Exhibitors and companion owners alike – that Salukis almost alone among the breeds vary enormously in type, and that each type is correct because it was evolved for special work in the special terrain frequented by the Tribe which evolved it.

Of course we all have our preferences, but these can be held without acrimony. The variation is mainly in size, but small or large, this must range within the standard 23 to 28 inches at the shoulder for dogs, with bitches proportionately smaller. As to detail, the most important are those already mentioned which the Bedouin Arab looks for and which are shown by the Arab imported hounds.

(a) The snout or muzzle must be long and narrow. This for breed.
(b) The girth at chest must be deep – the deeper the better. This for staying power.
(c) The girth at waist must be fine. This for speed.
(d) The hocks must be well let down. This for speed.
(e) The width between the tops of the thigh bones measured on the back must be good, i.e. at least the width of a hand including thumb. This for speed.

For the rest, the dog with two hair warts under the chin is better than that with only one, and the one having three or four such hair warts is very good.

Saluki or Gazelle Hound Club

The Saluki or Gazelle Hound Club was founded in 1923, with the Honourable Florence Amherst (Amherstia) as its first President.

The first declared object of the Club was "To promote the breeding of Salukis by endeavouring to make the qualities of the breed better known; and also to encourage the exhibition of Salukis by procuring classes for them at some of the leading dog shows in different centres throughout the country and giving special prizes."

Today, fifty years later, these objects can be said to have been achieved: at least 15 Championship Shows each year and an increasing number of Open Shows schedule the breed, apart from 3 Shows exclusively for Salukis run by the Club itself. These are: a Limited Show around the first week in June for members only, an Open Show in the 3rd week in July in conjunction with the Arab Horse Show, and the Saluki Championship Show where Challenge Certificates are awarded usually sometime in September. In addition, informative Rallies are held from time to time, and a twice-yearly magazine is well supported.

As regards promoting the breeding of Salukis, the stage has now been reached where, again taking a leaf from the Arab's book, it is important to be much more selective in our breeding programmes. As already mentioned, very few Saluki litters in England are culled, as the Arabs do. Consequently too many people who buy bitches are breeding litters without very much knowledge of what is involved or sufficient experience of the breed to discern a good specimen from a bad. It follows that these litters are often hard to dispose of and the Saluki puppies get into the hands of people who admire their beauty but cannot cope with their characters as hounds and fast moving hounds at that. Or else unscrupulous owners acquire them for crossing with the modern Kelb and thus destroy the breed. The sad result is too often an unhappy Saluki in a bad or unsuitable home.

So, on the proposal of the President Mrs H.M. Parkhouse, the Rule 19 has now been changed to read "To ensure the continued purity of the breed." In pursuance of this, every effort is made throughout the club to spread "knowledge of the breed" and share the collective experience of the membership. A special feature of the Club is a rescue scheme for any Saluki known to be in trouble and an automatic third party insurance built in to Members' subscriptions.

According to the rules originally laid down, the Club is run by a President, a Vice President and a Committee. These are elected annually by a secret ballot. The President is automatically the chairman at all meetings, but because he or she may not always be able to be present, the Committee for administrative convenience elects a Chairman of Committee and appoints a Secretary and Treasurer.

On the death of the first President Miss Amherst, the late Lady Gardner (Knightellington) became President and she was followed by Lady Baddeley. At the time of writing, Mrs H.M. Parkhouse (of Shammar) is President of the Club and the Vice President is Mrs Helen Baker — daughter of Lady Gardner who has inherited her mother's Knightellington prefix and maintains the quality of this well known strain with considerable distinction. Brigadier General Lance was the first Chairman of Committee and Mrs Lance was Secretary for many years and worked very hard for the Club. It was General and Mrs Lance who were mainly instrumental in getting Salukis recognised by the Kennel Club and in forming the Saluki Club itself.

The Saluki Club is registered with the Kennel Club and obeys its rules. The Kennel Club governs everything to do with Pedigree dogs, as the Jockey Club governs Horse Racing. During the War, the Saluki Club, like so many others, went so to speak into hibernation. It owes a lot for its survival to Mr H.B. Parkhouse, now Honorary Vice President, who as Secretary and Treasurer combined kept all the paper work going and the subscriptions collected throughout the war.

The Saluki Club now has around 400 members including 70 overseas members. It also has a flourishing coursing section which aims at preserving the hunting qualities of the breed especially in the show specimens through the exercise of this ancient and historic sport.

The Club runs three Saluki specialist Shows annually including a Championship Show. Several informative but informal Rallies are also held. Members at the time of writing are sent the Saluki Club Magazine twice yearly.

All Saluki owners are cordially advised to apply for membership of the Saluki or Gazelle Hound Club and this is specially true for any who have owned Salukis in the lands of their origin and who may be able to bring first-hand knowledge of present day desert conditions and perhaps new and imported Saluki blood.

The address of the Secretary of the Saluki Club can always be obtained from the Kennel Club, 1, Clarges Street, Piccadilly, London W.1. who will also give names and addresses of some of the principal breeders. At the time of writing, the Secretary of the Saluki Club is Mrs Joan McLeish — "Grove House", Watton Road, Knebworth, Herts.